Praise F
FIVE MINUTES

"The Sandler Selling System has helped multi-product, VITO-closing powerhouse, ope... globe and grow revenues over 500% over the past four years. looking for similar results you need to read this book."

— John Clancy, President, *Iron Mountain Digital*

"David and Tony are a great team. Profoundly simple advice and simply masterful. Read, internalize and your success will materialize."

— Dr. Denis Waitley, author of *The Seeds of Greatness*

"This book answers the first question that pops into the heads of most VITOs: 'How long will this take?' Kudos to Tony and David for providing excellent answers to questions so many sales pros face on a daily basis."

— Tom Hopkins, author of *How to Master the Art of Selling*

"Wow! Here is a great book that shows you how to make more and bigger sales -- at a higher level than you may have thought possible."

— Brian Tracy, author of *The Psychology of Selling*

"Tony and David have written a winner in *'Five Minutes with VITO!'* The insights shared will help any sales professional close more sales faster! Don't miss this one!"

— Don Hutson, co-author of the #1 New York Times bestseller, *The One-minute Entrepreneur*

"What a great partnership: Sandler Training and VITO Selling. That's a better combo than peanut butter and chocolate! This book is very easy to read, with numerous 'take-it-to-the-bank' ideas."

— Dr. Tony Alessandra, author of *The Platinum Rule* and *Charisma*

"*Five Minutes with VITO* combines the two best in the business: Sandler and VITO."

— Joe Mancuso, Founder of *CEO Club, www.ceoclub.org*

"Tony Parinello once again reinforces his claim as one of the top sales experts in the world with *Five Minutes with VITO*. These pages contain your roadmap to 'Sales Paradise' -- just follow the trail."

— Warren Greshes, author of *The Best Damn Sales Book Ever*

"This is the definitive book on how to flip the 'switch' in the decision maker's mind that you previously thought unflippable."

— Pete Montoya, author of *The Brand Called You*

FIVE MINUTES WITH VITO

David Mattson
and
Anthony Parinello

PEGASUS
Media World

Publisher
Pegasus Media World
PO Box 7816
Beverly Hills, CA 90212

For further information please visit www.sandler.com or call: 1-800-638-5686, or visit www.sellingtovito.com or call: 1-800-777-VITO

Five Minutes with VITO: Making the most of your selling time with the Very Important Top Officer
© 2009 Sandler Systems, Inc. and Anthony Parinello
ISBN, print ed. 978-0-9786078-3-8

Cover design: Mike Davis

First Printing: 2009

Publisher's Cataloging-in-Publication

Mattson, David, 1963-
Five minutes with VITO: making the most of your selling time with the very important top officer / David Mattson, Anthony Parinello. — 1st ed.
p. cm.
Includes index.
LCCN 2008928457
ISBN-13: 978-0-9786078-3-8
ISBN-10: 0-9786078-3-X

1. Selling. 2. Chief executive officers.
I. Parinello, Anthony. II. Title. III. Title: Maximize your selling time with the very important top officer.

HF5438.25.M38 2008   658.85

QBI08-600146

In memory of
David H. Sandler

೫೫ ೫೫

David H. Sandler

(November 4, 1930 – September 13, 1995)

Dedication

David H. Sandler was the creator of the Sandler Selling System® and founder of the Sandler Sales Institute in 1967. He created and perfected a replicable sales training program with his no pressure, nurturing selling style that has forever transformed the landscape of professional selling.

As you read this book you will be given a unique glimpse and learn directly from David Sandler's personal Attitude-Behavior journals. David Sandler's wisdom and his insights are inscribed at the beginning of each chapter and throughout the book.

David Sandler taught us the true purpose of Life-long learning and the profound importance of ongoing reinforcement of our learning through taking action, accepting personal accountability and continually asking for help.

All of the Sandler Training℠ employees and franchisees worldwide who knew David Sandler personally or knew him indirectly through repeated listening and studying of his audio recordings invite you to use what you learn from this book in your day-to-day professional sales and management career and your personal life as well.

And maybe a little piece of David Sandler will find its way into your own life, too.

About Dave Mattson
CEO, Sandler Systems, Inc.

Dave Mattson is the CEO and a partner at Sandler Systems, Inc., an international training and consulting organization. Since 1986, he has been a trainer and business consultant in management, sales, interpersonal communication, corporate team building and strategic planning throughout the United States and Europe. His domestic and international clients include top-name organizations in many different industries.

An early lesson in goal orientation came when Dave was a child in Connecticut. When snow fell and school was cancelled, Dave shoveled driveways for pay – and would have contests with other shovelers to see who could clear out the most driveways by the end of the day. He noticed that the days when he had contests with other people were invariably days when he made the most money. The lesson: Setting a goal (such as winning a contest) equates to higher sales production. This was the first of many lessons on the psychology of sales, a topic that has been a passion of Dave's for many decades.

Dave's consulting and training experience encompasses a wide range of sales and management topics designed to increase the productivity and efficiency of any company. Participants and clients often describe his creative enthusiasm, problem solving and curriculum design as particular strengths. He met Sandler Training founder David Sandler in 1986, fell in love with his material, went to work for Mr. Sandler in 1988, and was eventually chosen to lead the company. His mission is to "help people make their lives better by using the Sandler approach."

About Tony Parinello
Founder and CEO, VITO Selling

In 1995, Tony Parinello started a revolution with his first best-selling book, *Selling to VITO, the Very Important Top Officer.* He's authored seven wildly successful sales books, personally trained over 2,000,000 salespeople and the majority of the Fortune 1000, and reaches salespeople around the world with his weekly Internet broadcasts. Tony's students learn to use his unique appointment-setting methods to present their ideas to CEOs, presidents, owners and other difficult-to-reach individuals who hold the ultimate veto power over all decisions made within their enterprises.

Tony's sales career started in 1978 and he is still very much in the game, making sales calls to VITOs on a regular basis. He didn't always do that, though.

Early in his career, he found a great deal of business at lower levels within organizations in his sales territory – in a place he now calls Linoleumville. This is the part of the organization where the folks that did the recommending had to fit their recommendations into a "budget." After three consecutive years of above quota sales performance, he created a very unfortunate situation: he was at 19% of quota, and the year was half over. As a result, his manager put him on probation. After the initial panic, and after realizing the "blame game" wasn't going to get him anywhere, he took stock and figured that if he was going to keep his job, he had to change the way he was selling. He booked a one-way ticket out of Linoleumville, started selling to VITO, and went from 19% to 103% of quota. The good news: He got to keep his job. The better news for salespeople around the world: He eventually left that company...and started the VITO selling revolution.

David's dedication:

To David H. Sandler, who created the greatest sales and management system in the marketplace.

David's acknowledgements:

To Bruce Seidman for sharing a common vision for Sandler. To the home office staff for all your hard work and dedication in making Sandler the most effective training/consulting company in the world. I would like to especially thank Rachel Miller, Steve Howell, and Howard Goldstein for their tireless attention to this project. To the Sandler trainers around the world who bring life and passion to David Sandler's message. And a special thanks to my family for their unconditional love and support.

Tony's dedication:
To George Vafis
a best friend who loved life, the sea and me.

Tony's acknowledgements:
Grateful thanks go out to…my entire team of top performers: Miki Davis, Mike Davis, Richard Hamilton, Beth Allen, Steve Dailey, Tad Shull, and Brandon Toropov – thank you all for being who you are and doing what you do…Nance Rosen and her team of marketing experts at Pegasus Media World, for helping us to get this book into your hands… all the VITO alumni and clients, who keep me growing and learning…the good folks at Sandler, for helping me bring my intellectual work to the next level…and you, whether you are a new friend or one of long standing, for your willingness to make sales history with me.

TABLE OF CONTENTS

Part Two: Set... / 57

Part Three: Go! / 99

PART ONE:
READY…

Should you read this book?

Permit us to begin our answer to that question by offering you two definitions of two very different places: *the Sales Graveyard* and *Sales Paradise.*

The Sales Graveyard is crammed full of sales that never happened, sales that were stopped dead in their tracks. Mind you, the salespeople trying to make those sales worked their behinds off: They did everything they were told to do, they jumped enthusiastically through all the hoops they were supposed to jump through, they did all the demos, presentations, and analyses they were told to do…and they still didn't make the sale.

At least, that's what *usually* happened. Sometimes (but not nearly often enough) the salesperson actually *did* make a sale. But those sales were generally a whole lot smaller than they could have been…and a whole lot slower in coming.

The occupants of the Sales Graveyard tend to have a ghostly appearance. They rattle their chains in an endless and vain search for the true Decision Maker. They walk for long, sleepless weeks in a quest for budgets that either disappear or never existed in the first place. They dig for information that is buried so deep that they can never find out what's actually going on in the organization. This is all familiar terrain for the residents of the Sales Graveyard. They have been condemned to live in this "shadow world" day in and day out – not once, with a single prospect, but regularly, with *most or all* of their prospects.

Does any of this sound even remotely relevant to your world? Good. That's all we need to get started. If you agree with us that the Sales Graveyard a) exists and b) is not where you really want to live…keep reading.

Sales Paradise is a very different place. Sales Paradise is a place where good things happen often and quickly. It's a place where salespeople exchange ideas, efforts, and ongoing good will with prospects and customers who do precisely the same things in turn. It's a place where the universal law of reciprocity works to the benefit of salespeople. It's a place where you deal with individuals who actually have the power, control, and authority to invest in you and your solutions. It's a place where top decision makers are willingly involved in the sales process. In Sales Paradise, sales cycles are short, entry-point orders are huge, and add-on orders materialize easily and with great frequency. High-quality referrals come your way effortlessly and they come your way as a matter of course.

That's Sales Paradise. Once you take up residence there you never want to live anywhere else. Sales managers love salespeople who have a zip code in Sales Paradise…and so do all the people who operate above sales managers, like vice presidents, presidents, CEOs, and owners. Salespeople who operate in Sales Paradise can afford to buy lots of goodies. Selling and living large is a way of life in Sales Paradise – and life there is definitely good!

This book, which is the product of nearly a century of experience on the sales front lines and in the sales training industry will get you to, and keep you in Sales Paradise *forever!*

The methods, mindsets, tactics, strategies, and advice you'll find on each page have been battle-tested by more than 15 million salespeople and more than one million organizations. The principles have been tested in virtually every industry that employs professional salespeople… and in every industry those salespeople sell to.

This is no joke. The program you will find outlined in this book *really works*. It is a ticket out of the Sales Graveyard and into Sales Paradise.

But…there's a catch.

In order to take advantage of what follows, you must be willing to take personal responsibility not just for what you *do,* but also for *what you believe* about yourself. In order to take advantage of what follows, you must be personally accountable for both what you do *and* what you believe on a day-to-day basis.

Who will you be accountable *to?*

That's easy. You.

Not your sales manager. Not the president of your company. Not your pal in Marketing. Not your mom. Not your dad. Not your eccentric Uncle Joe.

You.

For any of this to work, you must be fully accountable…*to yourself*… for what you actually do and actually think, today and each and every day of your sales career. Right now, for instance. Now, here's why you should sign on with us, catch or no catch.

If you choose to follow our lead and choose to do *all* the activities we give you, you will find that becoming personally accountable *to yourself* will be easy, not hard, to do. As a result, your income, your quality of life and your ability to have a good time will all be enhanced.

By the same token, if you choose *not* to follow the program we lay out for you here, this book will almost certainly be a complete waste of your time and money.

Knowing what you now know, you should answer the question "Should I read this book?" For yourself. You should either proceed to the (virtual or physical) checkout, buy the book, and get started…or stop reading, take this book out of your (virtual or physical) shopping cart, and forget all about it.

It's all up to you.

You're still with us, so congratulations. You're about to go on a wild, deeply enjoyable ride.

At this point, people typically ask us two questions.

Question number one is: "Who is this VITO I supposedly want get five minutes with?" *Answer:* VITO is the Very Important Top Officer, the person with the ultimate "veto power," the person with final say on all the decisions that are made in the enterprise. VITOs typically have titles like CEO, president, owner, and company founder.

Question number two is: "Do you really expect me to try to land my first appointment with the Very Important Top Officer at my target company?" *Answer:* Yes.

Perhaps you remember what we said to you earlier about account-ability. It's time to start putting that into action. You will find an important question in the paragraph immediately below this one. **Read the question and answer it honestly, out loud.**

Right now, do you believe that you have ANYTHING IN COMMON *with the VITOs in your territory and the world at large — with the CEOs, presidents, company owners, and company founders?*

Again: Answer that question honestly, and answer it out loud, so you can physically hear your own response.

If your answer was "yes" or even "maybe," you're now officially ready for this book. If that wasn't your answer, change it. You have a lot in common with these folks, and we will prove it to you in the following pages.

Before we get started in earnest, let us share a promise with you and set some expectations.

First, the promise. We will never ask you to do anything we don't do ourselves...day after day, week after week, quarter after quarter. Yes, we both sell for a living, just like you. When we ask you to do some-thing, we know from personal experience that what we are advocating works across multiple industries. You don't have to worry that you're going to be a guinea pig in somebody's research project. Not only that: Everything we ask you to do will be ethical, legal, and (this is the important part) *do-able.*

Even though the things we suggest may occasionally seem to be beyond your comfort zone, we can also promise you this: You *can* do it...and once you internalize the activity and start taking responsibility for doing it yourself, you can use it to deliver much better results than you're getting right now.

"Better results" means specifically: better information, faster selling cycles, larger entry-point orders, more repeat business, and referrals that are worth considerably more than their weight in gold. In other words, Sales Paradise.

Now, here's what we expect from you: we want you to read each chapter in sequence, starting with this introduction, and then put what you learn into play as you go along. We expect you to get off the bench, step into the game, and immediately take action to close the gap between what you *know* and what you actually *do and think*. Specifically, we expect you to take the *Action Steps* we will be giving you at the end of selected chapters. Here comes your very first Action Step. Look how easy it is!

ACTION STEP

Move quickly to Chapter One.

CHAPTER ONE

"Luck is preparation meeting opportunity."
– David Sandler

Meet VITO,
the Very Important Top Officer...
and Everyone Else

Who is VITO?

Once again: VITO is the Very Important Top Officer.

VITO is the captain of the ship.

VITO is the person with the ultimate power, control, influence, and authority over everything that takes place in the organization. As the name suggests, VITO has the ultimate veto power. Period. When we talk about VITO, we're talking about the CEO, the president, the owner, the chairperson of the board, the mayor, the governor, the general, the tribal chief, the top cop, the chancellor, the dean of schools, the head honcho, the big dog, the top banana, the Big Kahuna.

There is a VITO in each and every account in your sales territory that you want to sell to, or are currently selling to. Building a good relationship with that VITO is the sales equivalent of the holy grail. It's what everyone is (or should be) looking for.

Over the years, some of the salespeople that we train have insisted that VITOs can have "lesser" titles like CFO, CIO, CTO, CMO, and other "C-suite" titles...or even titles like Vice-President of Marketing. Typically, these same salespeople try to convince us on this point by providing what they feel is "social proof" to substantiate their claim.

We hear things like, "The real VITO doesn't much care about what I sell." Or, "VITO has gatekeepers that nobody could possibly get past, so I don't try to sell there." Or, "The people I call on are the ones who sign my contract, and that's what counts."

What's your opinion? Do you feel the best individuals to contact are VITO's direct reports – or VITO? Have you ever *tried* to reach out to make an appointment with VITO, only to be shunted to someone with a different – let's face it, lesser – title? Did you then *stop* trying to make contact at the top of the enterprises you were trying to sell to?

The best way to find out whether you now have the proper target in your prospective accounts is to take the following brief test. Of course, like all other diagnostic tests, this one is meaningless if you don't answer it honestly. (By the way, this is the part where you start being accountable to yourself. Take the test and tell the truth – not for us, but for you.)

1. Have you ever lost a sale…after being told by your contact that you had *won* the sale? __Yes __No

2. Have you ever been told by your contact that he or she was making the decision… and *didn't want you contacting anyone else* in the organization? __Yes __No

3. Did your contact ever assure you that he or she was the one making the decision…and, later on in the process, learn that he or she had to get budget approval, or any kind of approval, *from someone else?* __Yes __No

4. Do you have any accounts that you feel you should be getting add-on business from… business you're *not getting?* __Yes __No

5. When you're meeting with your current contact…are you standing on *linoleum?* __Yes __No

If you've just answered "yes" to even one of these questions, we have bad news and good news to share with you. The bad news is that you're *not selling in the right place!* The good news is that we can teach you how to transform your thoughts and actions.

To do that, though, we must get very clear on who you want to sell to…and why.

There are four very different levels of influence and authority in today's enterprise. The people operating at the various levels *don't* have equal amounts of influence and authority.

What Do You Mean by Influence and Authority?

Glad you asked. Take a look at these definitions.

> *Influence:* **Having the ability to change the minds and thinking patterns of others. Being able to introduce new ideas with confidence and credibility.**

> *Authority:* **Having the ability to make decisions and allocate any amount of financial, political, and/or human resources that are required to achieve one's goal.**

What level of influence and authority have you been selling to? To answer that question, let's take a journey through today's enterprise and let's start at the highest point.

Level One. At the top of every organization there is one leader, one person with *the* vision. This is the player with the *ultimate* influence and authority, the person who cares the most about seemingly disparate topics like revenues cost containment, compliance, shareholder value and brand reputation in the marketplace. This is the one person to whom everyone and everything in the organization is accountable. We will always call the person holding this critical position VITO, *the Very Important Top Officer.* VITO is the only one who's responsible for every aspect of the enterprise. At the end of the day, VITO holds the score card. Win, lose or draw, VITO must play with whatever deal has gone down. VITO is the ultimate Approver of absolute everything that happens at VITO, Inc., including your sale.

As you can imagine, VITO has a heck of a lot to do. Too much, in fact. As a result, VITO empowers other individuals to make sure the job gets done. That takes us to the next level down.

Level Two. One level below VITO you'll find the individuals VITO trusts the most in the organization to do exactly what VITO wants to get done in exactly the way VITO would do it: with the utmost effectiveness, efficiency, cost-awareness, schedule-awareness, and success-awareness. These hand-picked, trusted advisors are typically politically astute. They are upwardly mobile. They are specialists in their area of responsibility. And they are *extremely* loyal to whatever cause VITO is excited about. That makes these individuals "yes-people." That's right! They get paid to say "yes" to VITO. In fact, if they want to keep their high-paying jobs, they *must* say "yes." Saying "yes" and then following through is, after all, what gets the things done that VITO wants done. We'll always call this group of trusted advisors *Decision Makers.*

Close-up on VITO, Inc.

VITO wants to take a whole new pharmaceutical marketplace by storm. VITO wants to catch the competition off-guard. VITO wants to capture some early-on market share. So – VITO calls a special meeting of all the Decision Makers at VITO, Inc. As VITO tells the story of what's going to happen, eyes and minds are wide open. Lots of notes are taken. Each and every one of those Decision Makers begins to understand the role he or she must play in this new initiative. The CFO must think about new areas of cost, about reallocation of financial resources, about compliance. The COO must under-stand how best to ramp up production. The CMO must come up with new ideas for packaging and, of course, new ideas for winning market share. The VP of Sales must hire, recruit, and retain critical sales resources. While all of these thoughts are going through peoples' minds...*everyone is saying yes!* All heads are nodding, all hands are sporting thumbs-up, all parties are in agreement. There is no doubt in anyone's mind. The new manufacturing, marketing, and sales initiatives connected to this pharmaceutical will be pursued aggressively, and it will deliver massive success to VITO, Inc.! You couldn't begin to *count* the number of "yes" answers VITO gets during this meeting. Each high-ranking person in the room is saying "yes" in support of VITO's new vision.

If any one of those high-ranking folks *were* to doubt VITO's cause...if any one of them *were* to be unsupportive...that would be what is known as a "career limiting" mistake.

That's the rule of the road for VITO: Decision Makers with unsupportive attitudes will not be tolerated...and can be easily replaced!

Level Three. Okay. What's going on at the next level down? Well, we know that Decision Makers are pretty busy people too, what with all the on- and off-site meetings, planning sessions, strategy meetings, focus groups, brainstorming panels, and of course, that all-important face time with VITO. These folks have to keep their hands on the pulse of all projects of importance and that's quite a job. In fact, it's *such* a big job that they need their own set of people *they* can turn to. These all-important advisors to the Decision Makers tend to be expert information gatherers, specialists in particular areas, problem solvers and trouble-shooters extraordinaire. They bring boatloads of experience to the job. We'll always call these people *Influencers*. They may be researchers, engineers, or scientists. They're likely to be "process people," experts in organizing and measuring things, who are well suited to dealing with tasks, projects, and deadlines. Decision Makers rely on these detail-oriented folks to provide an objective eval-uation of whatever problem may be thrown their way. There are two interesting things we've noticed over the years about these folks. First, Influencers always want to "see more" charts, data, recommendations, product specs, and so on from salespeople. So much so that they've earned a nickname: Seemore. Second, Influencers tend to occupy offices, labs, and conference rooms whose floors are covered, not with the plush carpet you'll find in VITO's office, but with *linoleum*.

Something to consider: How much time are you spending in Linoleumville with Seemore?

Close-up on VITO, Inc.

Seconds after all the Decision Makers at that huge pharmaceutical firm left VITO's special meeting, they started sprinting to their offices. Why? Because they had to call special meetings of their own! The CFO called in the accountants, buyers, and purchasing agents. The COO called in the materials manager and plant operations manager. The CMO called in the media agency, the market consultant, and the product marketing manager. The VP of Sales called in all the area sales managers and the head of sales training.

Here's what happened: Each and every one of those Decision Makers said something like this to the team: *"Guess what? We've got new marching orders from the top. We are releasing a new pill that will take the marketplace by storm! I want each and every one of you to find out exactly what it will take for us to get this job done – to VITO's standards, ahead of time, and under budget."* Then, the Decision Makers all handed out assignments.

Each meeting concluded with the Decision Maker making a solemn promise: "There will be no slip-ups. There will be no missed deadlines. We are going to do what VITO wants, and we are going to do it right. We will have weekly status reports, and each of you will let me know what's going on…and how we're actually doing against the timeline and goals VITO has set for us."

As the Influencers left the meeting, some were thinking to

themselves: *"I've already got way too much on my plate. How am I going to find the time to get this done?"* Others were thinking, *"This is great. I'll get the chance to do a complete and thorough evaluation of all of the possible (yap, yap, blah, blah) providers. I love doing complete and thorough evaluations of things."* (You can fill in the "yap, yap, blah, blah" with the name of the products and services you sell). And still others were muttering: *"Wow. He said 'no slip-ups!' I've got to get a committee together so we can look into this and figure out all the possible ramifications of what we're trying to do."* Did someone say "committee?" That takes us to the next, and lowest level in the enterprise.

Level Four. The individuals who make up this population may be called rank and file employees. They typically assemble, support, expedite, inspect, repair, sell, account for, and service whatever is being created, manufactured, re-sold, grown, or produced by VITO, Inc. They may sit on committees, too.

These folks make great members of focus groups or user groups, because they generally know the most about the day-to-day operations at VITO, Inc. They are, generally speaking, the people who are most likely to actually use whatever it is you happen to be selling. That means they're well suited for making recommendations about what might and might not work. We'll always call this group of people *Recommenders*.

From time to time, Influencers call upon Recommenders to perform various intricate tests and evaluations. Typically, Influencers want to overcome all the possible problems and, ultimately, get the "buy-in" of Recommenders. They want to make sure that all the bases are covered. And who knows more about what bases need to get tagged and when, than the Recommenders?

If you have ever provided a "sample" or "loaner" of what you sell, the chances are excellent that whatever you loaned to your prospect was given to a Recommender or a group of Recommenders.

If you look at virtually any well-run organization in the world, you'll find the four groups we've just identified. The question is – who's going to be your contact at VITO, Inc.?

Wait! Don't answer that yet. Instead, do the Action Step that follows.

Be ruthlessly honest, otherwise there's absolutely no point to any of this. Write the answers down in the space provided.

ACTION STEP

Over the past 90 days, how many:

VITOs have you met with personally?

Decision Makers have you met with personally?

Influencers have you met with personally?

Recommenders have you met with personally?

CHAPTER TWO

"Decide what you want, build a plan, and you can bet on the outcome." – David Sandler

Why Sell to VITO?

Question...

What did you learn about your selling process from the "action step" at the end of the last chapter? Over the past 90 days who were you spending most of your time with?

If you're like most of the people we work with, you concluded that you spent most of your face time with Influencers and Recommenders, and perhaps some time with Decision Makers as well. It's likely, however, that you spent little or no time with VITO. In fact, unless you've already had some kind of contact with the VITO selling philosophies, you probably didn't start *any* of your sales cycles with VITO.

And that's a shame because these days VITO's office is where all the interesting decisions are made.

Over the past three decades, there's been a fascinating and somewhat disturbing organizational change. Perhaps you've noticed it too. "Signature levels" of authority have continued to climb *up* the corporate organizational chart. At the very same time the dollar amount that individuals who aren't VITO can approve on their own has *declined*.

In other words, the folks that you sold to in the past can't really buy from you in the present...unless you've lowered your price points!

Of course, your contacts won't tell you this. They're not particularly proud of the fact that, five or ten years ago, they used to be able to sign off on and spend as much as $250,000, but can now only sign off on and spend say $2,500 tops, without running the decision past VITO. That's literally true of Decision Makers these days, at least in our experience.

Unfortunately, most sales processes have not been modified to reflect this increasingly obvious fact of corporate life. Your sales process, however, *must* change…if you hope to enter Sales Paradise.

There are a lot of uncertainties in the world of sales today but you can take this fact to the bank: Trying to sell to someone *with* a need who can't actually buy from you will yield the same result as trying to sell to someone who can buy but *doesn't have the need.* The outcomes are going to be precisely the same: No sale, no commission, no quota credit.

"Yeah, but VITOs don't buy what I sell!"

No – they don't! As a matter of fact, they couldn't care less about what you sell. They do, however, have a sincere and vested interest in what your product, service, or solution can do for their top, middle and/or bottom lines. If you don't believe that…consider this story.

Back when he was selling computer systems, Tony Parinello was sitting in the office of the president of a jet-engine manufacturer. Today was a special day: the first shipment on a major contract. The president's office had one wall with floor-to-ceiling windows that looked out over the manufacturing facility. That gave anyone in the room, including Tony, a bird's eye view of the whole operation. It was very impressive!

Earlier that day, while he was out on the floor, Tony had seen the COO walking in the manufacturing area. One of the facility managers had been mopping up a spill. "Everything okay, Jake?" the COO had asked. "You bet, boss," Jake had answered, still mopping. "Getting ready for the big day!" Without looking back, the COO gave Jake a big thumbs-up.

That was an hour and a half earlier. Tony's meeting with the CEO was going to be a brief one and it had only two agenda items:

congratulate the president on purchasing the computer system that he had signed off on, and plant the seed for the next phase of the business relationship.

Just minutes after Tony's meeting with the Big Kahuna started, though, he heard a loud crash from down on the factory floor. Seconds later, he saw all the lights on the phones on the president's desk start pulsing like warning lights on the control panel of a space vehicle that was experiencing a major malfunction.

The president punched a button, picked up the line, and said, "Hello?...What the hell...I'll be right there." Before Tony could get out of his chair, the president had run to the windows that looked out over the factory floor. "Holy Moses!" the president said. (Okay, he didn't really say that; he actually said something considerably more interesting. But "Holy Moses" will help us comply with contemporary business book publishing standards!)

What Tony saw when he looked out through the big windows was almost enough to make a grown man cry. A fork-lift had been moving the shiny, soon-to-be-delivered, first-off-the-floor jet engine. For some reason, the fork-lift had skidded out of control and sideswiped a 15-foot-rack of raw materials. The impact sent every last piece and part flying off the rack. The engine was now covered with metallic debris...and damaged. It would have to be repaired before it could be shipped.

Why did it happen? Well, it turned out that good old Jake – remember Jake? – was all out of the recommended cleaning solution for mopping up hydraulic spills. When the COO had passed by on the floor, Jake had been using some "off the shelf" stuff that left the floor *looking* clean but also left it as slick as ice for any unsuspecting fork-lift driver who might be passing by, bearing 5,000 or so pounds of brand-new jet engine.

In an eye-blink, VITO was faced with a major non-compliance delivery crisis – all because a fifteen-dollar bottle of cleaning solution had not been available.

Now let us ask you a question. Does VITO buy cleaning supplies?

No. VITO doesn't give a flaming hoot about cleaning supplies.

But you can bet that VITO definitely *does* care about non-compliance delivery issues, and about keeping new customers who place orders for jet engines satisfied!

If your cleaning solution connects to those issues in any way – and after that story, we're thinking it probably does – then you should be spending your first five minutes with VITO. Ask yourself: *What would happen to VITO's organization if my product, service, or solution suddenly weren't available, and/or was replaced by an inferior substitute?*

19 Really, Really Good Reasons to Sell to VITO

As far as we're concerned, the "Brand X Cleaning Solution" story is reason enough to start your process at the top. In case you need additional reasons, though, here are nineteen more of them:

1. *VITOs are impatient and intolerant about delays of any sort.* They like people who know how to step on the gas. We've yet to meet a VITO who wants to wait any longer than is absolutely necessary to realize improvements and/or accomplishments of their goals, plans, or objectives. Basically, VITOs live for instant gratification. When they see something they want, they make arrangements to get it very, very quickly. Quite often, VITOs will want to buy what you have and get their hands on it faster than you can deliver it. Think about what that means for your selling cycle.

2. *VITO lives in a world of abundance and sees the world as a massive garden of opportunity.* Everything is bigger in VITO's world. When you interact with VITOs, you quickly realize that their offices are bigger, their desks are bigger, and yes, their vision is bigger. Therefore, when they buy, they buy (you guessed it) BIG! That means your average sale size increases.

3. *VITO wants improvements in every area of their enterprise.* Once you deliver the value you've promised, you'll find that VITO will want to see your solutions across departmental lines. In other words, you'll get all the add-on business you've worked hard for and deserve!

4. *Unlike other people in the organization (notably Influencers) VITOs love to make decisions.* VITOs know full well that nothing happens

until a decision is made, and they're not at all shy about making them. If a VITO makes a "wrong" decision...no worries, they'll get everything back on track by making better informed, more refined decisions. Stop and think: Who would you rather be playing with? Someone who relishes the act of making choices? Or someone who runs as fast as possible in the opposite direction of making a firm commitment?

5.   *VITO knows what's hot and what's not at any given moment.* VITO understands better than anyone in the organization what's really on the "to-do" list. And VITO keeps that list up-to-date! Furthermore, when the "hot list" changes, VITO is the first to know about it. Don't you want that person in your "loop?"

6.   *VITOs not only know who's who — they know who's doing what to whom!* VITO knows all the important players and movers and shakers within the entire enterprise. In fact, the various players in the enterprise are only important *if* VITO knows them! VITO can and will give immediate orders to those players. Wouldn't you prefer that VITO were the one ordering these folks to talk and meet with you?

7.   *VITO has no budget.* What VITO wants, VITO gets. Period. Isn't this the person you'd like to see wanting your stuff?

8.   *VITOs are the most direct people in the enterprise.* What's more, they hate to waste precious time. Therefore, VITOs won't pretend to be interested just to generate a "second set of numbers." They won't tell you that an opportunity exists when it really doesn't. By the same token, if there *is* an opportunity, they'll tell you exactly what you have to do to turn it into a reality. Doesn't that sound like a refreshing change of pace?

9.   *Most VITO's have an "early adopter" mindset: They want to be the person who has what no one else has.* Wouldn't you like to sell your cutting-edge products and services to folks like that?

10.   *VITO knows the importance of sales.* The adage "Nothing happens until somebody sells something" really rings true to VITO's ears. That's because, more than anyone else in the organization, VITO

knows the importance of new business revenue and market share. As if that weren't enough, VITO actually respects what you do for a living.

11. VITOs know other VITOs. Why does that matter in your world? Well, when you ask for a referral, VITO will almost always refer you to…another VITO. Birds of a feather really do flock together. The sooner you start calling on VITOs…the sooner you can start collecting these "golden referrals" that will bring you bigger deals in less time. This is a "cycle of success" if ever there was one.

12. VITOs love great new ideas. In fact, they're the only people in the whole organization who absolutely, positively won't be threatened by them. The very best person to give VITO a new idea is you. Think about it: if you're not putting every VITO in your sales territory on a constant diet of new ideas, guess who you have to assume is doing so? Your competition. And that's definitely not cool.

13. VITOs have a competitive spirit. Specifically, they love to win and hate to lose. Even if they don't even *want* what they just won…they hate the idea of losing it. What does that mean to you? It means, my friend, that VITO has a deep respect for people who are competitive enough to reach out to him or her. Also: if you're a top producer, or on your way to being one, you may well find VITO to be an important ally.

14. VITO can handle tough questions (when they're phrased respectfully) and will generally answer them. Not only that, VITO respects the people who *ask* tough questions. Ask VITO for an answer to virtually any business question…and ye shall receive!

15. VITO likes to look at the big picture and dislikes getting bogged down in the details. During a typical day at VITO, Inc., some people run into VITO and forget exactly who the're talking to, they ramble on and on and on. You won't, though. That means if you can get to the point, talk about something that actually matters and then shut up, you will very likely discover that you have a genuinely attentive and engaged conversational partner.

16. VITOs know they don't know everything…and they also know that the fastest way to success is through the knowledge of others. This has huge implications. VITOs are always trying to compensate for what they know they don't know…and will fill the knowledge gap with competent, qualified individuals. Why wouldn't you want to be one of those trusted advisors?

17. When VITOs makes a sales call, they call another VITO. Now think about this one for a minute. When VITO calls VITO, the VITO being called usually *doesn't* have the exact same title. You know what that means? It means "title-to-title" equivalency is not important, but rather functional equivalency matters. Like-minded individuals can (and do) build rapport quickly with VITO. You can be one of them.

18. VITOs are comfortable with risk. They know it's a part of life and an important part of business. They will make intelligent, informed decisions that include acceptable levels of risk…if they can justify doing so. That means they're among the most likely people in the enterprise to establish new alliances with companies like, let's say, yours.

19. Ready for the mind-blower? Roughly 85% of VITOs were once salespeople! Get used to this one, because we're going to be spending some time on it. You have much, much more in common with this person than you think. If for some reason you're still finding that hard to believe at a gut level, stick with us and we'll turn you into a believer.

ACTION STEP

In the spaces below, write down FIVE ADJECTIVES that you think most accurately describe VITO.

1.

2.

3.

4.

5.

CHAPTER THREE

"The professional never does anything by accident."
– David Sandler

Why Five Minutes?

So...

Now we know why we want to sell to VITO. The question that's on your mind now may sound like this – why not shoot for the stars? Why not plan, from the outset, on spending a couple of *hours* with VITO? Why focus so closely on the first five minutes of the relationship?

The answer is pretty simple: Because, when it comes to VITO, the first five minutes will either make you or break you…and your sale.

In fact, you can't even count on five minutes.

What you're about to read may be difficult to accept, but it is the brutal truth nevertheless: You should expect VITOs to decide whether it makes sense for them to even consider pursuing a business relationship with you in about *eight seconds*, max.

Now, eight good seconds with VITO may not seem like a particularly large time window to you, but we are here to tell you that you really can open the right doors in that period…if you strategize those eight seconds properly.

Actually, eight seconds is an eternity in VITO-land. Once you get good at making it past the eight-good-seconds threshold with VITO – and you will – five good minutes will begin to feel like spending the weekend at VITO's summer home. *But you have to be ready to make the most of the first eight seconds, the very instant they come your way.* You have to know exactly what you're doing in those critical opening seconds, what you're doing in the first minute, and what you're doing in the first five minutes. *And you have to have unshakeable confidence as you do it.*

Wow. Who else in the enterprise requires that kind of commitment from us? Who else do we have to prepare for with such precision and such economy? Who else gets to hold us to an eight-second standard?

Nobody.

That's because VITOs are a breed apart. If you try to "fake" the first few moments with anyone else in the organization, you may be able to recover. VITO demands a whole different game plan.

The standards for a conversation with VITO are higher than they are with anyone else in the enterprise. There's a good reason for that. VITOs set higher standards *for themselves* than anyone else in the enterprise! Not only that: As a general rule, VITOs only like building alliances with people who have the same level of confidence and sense of self-worth that they do. And they size up whether people have that level of confidence and self-reliance quickly. Not in hours. Not in minutes. But in seconds.

Now, follow this next part carefully. To make the most of those critical opening seconds, *you will need to know what makes VITO tick.* Fortunately, we know all about that topic, and we're willing to share what we know with you.

Recently, Tony interviewed more than 120 VITOs to create his best-selling book *Think and Sell Like a CEO.* The interviews took place in many different venues – from airport VIP lounges to prestige corner offices in New York City's financial district, from a sprawling pineapple ranch on the big island of Hawaii to a rustic farm house in Tuscany, Italy. Although the settings changed dramatically, what Tony discovered during his interviews with these high-flying folks remained remarkably consistent. VITO's are not only characters – they are *people* of character. They are driven by ten critical *values,* unshakable personal standards that shape everything they do. And they invariably display ten powerful *leadership traits.* To make the most of your eight seconds, your one minute, and your five minutes with VITO, *you must understand these values and these traits.* Make a promise to yourself. If you ignore them, or try to tap-dance your way around them, you will crash and burn.

Taken together, VITO's values and VITO's leadership traits are an expression of VITO's underlying sense of self, which is typically quite powerful – ten on a scale of one to ten. And VITO looks for allies who have that same "ten out of ten" way of looking at themselves.

Take a look at the ten guiding *values* that VITO's invariably display in their business dealings.

1. *Integrity.* They do what they say they're going to do, when they said they will do it. VITO's word means a lot.
2. *Honesty.* They are open with their communication – some might even say "blunt." VITOs tell it like it is.
3. *Trustworthiness.* They know how to protect relationships and maintain commitments. They are big on loyalty.
4. *Compassion.* They show concern, tend to empathize strongly with people they deal with, and have a sincere desire to understand situations and individuals.
5. *Congruency.* This is a fancy word that translates as "what you see is what you get." The VITO you observe at work is the VITO you see at home.
6. *Altruism.* They're big on giving back. They find a way to contribute in an unselfish and humane way, often anonymously.
7. *Persistence.* They do not give up.
8. *Pragmatism.* They don't mistake hope for facts.
9. *Self-assurance.* They believe completely in themselves and in the mission of their organizations.
10. *Faith.* They believe that there is a higher power, even though they may shy away from defining that higher power explicitly or discussing it with others. VITOs tend to be quietly devoted.

So. Those are the values that guide and support VITO's day. Now take a look at the *leadership traits* that drive all of VITO's business relationships.

1. *Competitive.* VITO's love to win and hate to lose. Period.

2. *Opinionated.* They "know what they know." They are ego-driven. They are highly outspoken and protective of their right to *be* outspoken.

3. *Brief and direct.* They are often perceived as being impatient or "short" with others. Another way to say this is VITOs are unfailingly "quick-minded" in their communications, and are likely to expect others to be the same way.

4. *Passionate.* These folks love to do what they do, and can sometimes seem downright fanatical about doing it.

5. *Knowledgeable.* They keep up with what's going on in a whole lot of different areas.

6. *Decisive.* They tend to make decisions quickly. They don't get stuck in the "paralysis of analysis."

7. *Creative.* They are always looking for a way to "build a better mouse trap." They don't let force of habit stand in the way of a good idea.

8. *Image-conscious.* They are mindful of their outward appearance and conscious of how they are likely to be perceived by others.

9. *Street-smart.* They look first for simple, easy-to-understand explanations and descriptions...and then test those explanations and decisions against conditions in the real world.

10. *Results-driven.* They love to measure progress. They live to set goals...and then over-achieve them.

Okay, it's time for the rubber to hit the road. You're going to start laying the foundation for your first eight seconds, your first one minute, and ultimately, your first five minutes with VITO...by identifying all possible areas you have in *common* with VITO.

Complete the Action Step that follows on the next page. And get ready for a surprise.

"Learn everything you can about your prospect." – David Sandler

ACTION STEP

a) Review the VALUES list closely. Then, in the space below, write down all the VALUES you already share with VITO.

b) Review the LEADERSHIP TRAITS list closely. In the space below, write down all the LEADERSHIP TRAITS you already share with VITO.

CHAPTER FOUR

"There is no growth without pain." – David Sandler

Attitudes and Latitudes

Suprised?

Did you take the time to make an honest inventory of the values and leadership traits you have in common with VITO at the end of the last chapter? If you skipped it, *be accountable to yourself* – and take the time to do it right now!

Our prediction is: If you've ever closed a sale, you were a "ten-out-of-ten." You had to be! To get that deal to move forward, you had to incorporate all ten VITO values! Think about it. Call to mind, right now, a specific sale you closed within the last sixty days – the bigger the better.

1. *Integrity.* In order to close that sale, you had to display character. You had to do exactly what you said you were going to do, when you said you were going to do it. Your word had to mean something. Otherwise, you wouldn't have gotten the deal.

2. *Honesty.* To close that sale, you had to be a straight shooter. You had to be forthright and direct about the consequences of *not* buying from you, and you had to be up-front about exactly what you could and couldn't do for the prospect. You had to "tell it like it is."

3. *Trustworthiness.* To close that sale, you had to protect relationships and maintain commitments. You had to put a premium on loyalty. Your prospect had to know they could trust you and your organization.

4. *Compassion.* To close that sale, you had to empathize with the person you were selling to. You had to show concern for that person, had to empathize strongly with the situations he or she faced.

5. *Congruency.* To close that sale, you couldn't send mixed messages. People had to witness a consistent message that what they saw from you really was what they were going to get.

6. *Altruism.* This may not connect to the sale you closed… and then again, it just may. The upper-tier sales producers we've worked with all find some way to give back to the community, whether that's through giving to the Make-a-Wish Foundation®, or by volunteering at a local shelter, or taking their kids to visit an old folks' home. Regardless of the method, they find some way to say to themselves (and to the world at large) "I'm not just in this for me." Sending that message is part of who they are…and part of what makes them respected by others.

7. *Persistence.* To close that sale, you kept coming back, reconnecting, finding new appropriate reasons to talk to the prospect about the various ways you could add value to his or her organization. Right?

8. *Pragmatism.* To close that sale, you had to be realistic – with yourself, your management and the prospect.

9. *Self-assurance.* To close that sale, you had to believe completely in yourself, your products, services, and solutions and in the mission of your organization.

10. *Faith.* Every one of us defines this tenth value element differently but my guess is that you, like VITO, have a connection to something larger than yourself, and that connection supports and sustains you in your sales work and your life.

Interesting, eh? When it comes to commonality with the values that drive VITO, you already have a heck of a lot in common with this person! Let's keep going. What about those VITO traits? Think once again about that big deal you closed. In order to land it, how did you take charge of the situation? In other words, how did you interact with other people, both inside and outside your own organization?

1. Were you *competitive*? Is it fair to say that you like coming in first? That you love to win and hate to lose?

2. In your own area of expertise, were you *opinionated*? Did you "know your stuff?" Were you willing to stand up for what you knew?

3. Were you *brief and direct*? Did you ever reach a point where you felt it was important to get straight to the point, to "cut to the chase?"

4. Were you *passionate*? Did you enjoy selling what you sold?

5. Were you *knowledgeable*? Did you have to keep up with what was going on in a whole lot of different areas, both inside and outside your own organization?

6. Were you *decisive*? Did you avoid getting stuck in the "paralysis of analysis?" Did you help others to avoid that trap?

7. Did you ever offer a *creative* solution? Did you find a way to move forward that no one else had thought of yet?

8. Were you *image-conscious*? Did you take into account how the prospect would perceive you and your organization?

9. Were you *street-smart*? Did you emphasize simple, easy-to-understand explanations and descriptions over "book learning?" Did you help set up ways to test your explanations and recommendations against conditions in the real world?

10. Were you *results-driven*? Were you focused on measuring progress – that is, your progress and the progress of other people – as you moved through the buying process? Did you help set up systems that would help people to measure the effectiveness of what you had sold them?

No doubt about it…when you are closing a big deal, *you already think and interact like VITO*. That's good news, because in order to operate at

VITO's latitude, you have to adopt VITO's attitudes.

What does this mean for you on a practical level? It means that, when you connect with VITO – in person, on the phone, on paper, or in any form of virtual communication, such as videoconferencing – you must speak, move, feel, and think *exactly the way you did when you closed the biggest deal that you ever closed in your life*. As the sale cycle moved forward, and all the way up to when you closed that deal, you were using all the values that you share with VITO, and you were taking full advantage of the traits you already have in common with VITO.

That's the "ten on a scale of ten" person you must be the minute you interact with VITO in any way, shape, or form.

Think of any world-class athlete – a defending Olympic champion, say, in the sport of your choice. As that athlete gets ready to compete in the biggest event of the Games, *he or she is visualizing success,* not fantasizing about everything that could go wrong. If all the training, all the workouts, all the special diets, all the talks with the trainer were executed perfectly in the weeks before the race but the athlete is thinking, "I'll never be able to do this," that athlete is not going to compete for gold! Why not? Because the athlete is sending the wrong message to the brain! If that's what's happening, something critically important is still missing from that person's game.

The successful athlete – and yes, the successful salesperson – visualizes the *best* game or sale he or she has ever run, not the worst. And that's what you need to do if you want to connect to VITO.

In this book, you're going to be learning a lot of **techniques** that will help you to connect with VITO…and make the very most of those critical five minutes. But none of those tactics will be of any use if your **attitude** and the resulting **behavior** don't send the message that you have been and are, throughout the relationship, entitled to act upon your *Equal Business Stature* with VITO.

> *"You can perform in your roles only in a manner consistent with how you see yourself conceptually."*
> *– David Sandler*

We'll explore this concept of Equal Business Stature in more depth in the next chapter. But before you go on, do the Action Step below.

ACTION STEP

a) Identify the single biggest deal you ever closed.

b) In the space below, write down the FIVE ADJECTIVES that most accurately describe how you felt when you closed that deal. Were you Overjoyed? Confident? Energized? Exuberant? Unstoppable? Use these, or pick your own adjectives.

CHAPTER FIVE

"If you are only what you were told you could be,
you're less than what you can be." – David Sandler

VITO's Headset

To recap...

Memorizing a list of **techniques** is not enough. You must adopt VITO's own **attitudes** (also known as "values") and **behaviors** (also known as "leadership traits") if you want to begin the sales process with VITO. In other words…you must clearly establish Equal Business Stature if you wish to sell your idea to VITO. You have a right to call VITO, you have a right to meet with VITO, you have a right to bounce an idea off VITO. And make no mistake, selling VITO *on your idea*, with unshakeable confidence, is what those first five minutes are going to be all about.

Now, most of the salespeople we train are initially very resistant to the idea of assuming that they ever could claim Equal Business Stature with VITO or that they can (or should) employ the same attitudes and behaviors that VITO employs on a daily basis. Common reasons for pushback on this point include:

- "I don't have VITO's title."
- "I don't have VITO's experience."
- "I don't have VITO's bank account."
- "I can't pretend to have more authority than I do."
- "I can't talk like VITO – it will sound like I'm being disrespectful."
- "I can't do this yet, but I'm going to work my way up to it later this quarter."

And on and on and on. Did any of those concerns escape your lips…or cross your mind? If so, let us ask you an important question.

Who, within the organization you're trying to sell to, talks like that? Who, within the organization you're trying to sell to, *thinks* like that? Look at it again:

"I don't… I don't… I don't…"

"I can't… I can't… I can't…"

It sure doesn't sound like VITO. And it doesn't sound much like the Decision Maker, either. At least, it doesn't sound like an *aspiring* Decision Maker. Let's think of those Decision Makers as "VITOs in training." When they get up in the morning and make their way into the bathroom, they take a deep breath and then look confidently into the mirror. And do you know who they see? VITO! During the course of the day that follows, Decision Makers do their level best to look, sound, act, and *think* the way VITO would look, sound, act, and *think!*

That whole "I don't…" and "I can't…" routine is most reminiscent of the *Influencer* – the person who's constantly finding flaws, assigning blame, explaining what can't possibly be done, and slowing things down. Was that really who you wanted to sound like? Is that really the person whose **attitude** you want to model when you pick up the phone to call VITO? Is that really the person whose **behavior** is going to help you build an alliance with the topmost person in the organization?

There is a selling principle so profound, and so simple, that we have devoted an entire page to it. Please look at the following page now and read that principle out loud.

When you approach a new prospect...you will be shunted to the person in the organization you SOUND THE MOST LIKE.

Think for a moment about exactly what that means. If you really want to spend your time with Influencers down in Linoleumville and initiate the sales cycle with them, then you should make an effort to sound as much like an Influencer as humanly possible.

As you do so, you should be sure to model the **attitudes** and **beliefs** of the Influencer. Once you have done that, you can rest assured that you'll be spending a whole lot of time with these folks…secure in the knowledge that somewhere, as you chat with the Influencer, a cold, dank, rectangular spot in the Sales Graveyard is being kept open just for you.

On the other hand, if you want to open the sales cycle with VITO, and initiate the sales cycle *there,* you should make an effort to sound as much like VITO as you possibly can! How do you do that? By assuming Equal Business Stature.

It should be obvious to you by now that if establishing Equal Business Stature is how VITO builds relationships, it should also be how *you* build relationships.

Are you going to establish Equal Business Stature with all due *respect?* Sure. VITO does that when it's time to connect with another VITO. Respect has to be the foundation of any and every discussion you have with VITO. Are you going to proceed with proper *forethought?* Absolutely. VITO does that. But when it comes to *subservience*…sorry. That's not in VITO's game plan, and it shouldn't be in yours, either.

A few more thoughts on Equal Business Stature are probably in order before we proceed. One of the key definitions of the word **stature** is "intellect." And "intellect" is, if you dig a little deeper, further defined as "understanding." Therefore, having equal stature means getting to an equal *level of understanding* with VITO. Here, based on that important idea, is a more complete definition of Equal Business Stature for you to consider.

EQUAL BUSINESS STATURE MEANS...having an equal understanding with VITO, of what some of VITO's most critical business interests and objectives are...and then being able to articulate and introduce thoughts, questions, and ideas about how you might be able to help to further or overachieve any one of those business interests or objectives.

In short, having Equal Business Stature means you are the functional equivalent of VITO. As such, you have the right, and the duty, to:

- Introduce new thoughts.
- Ask direct questions.
- Become a trusted advisor.
- And, yes, change VITO's thought process!

Your title doesn't matter. Whether or not you feel ready for this right now doesn't matter. *All that matters is whether you have an idea that connects to VITO's interests and objectives.*

So, if you want to create this relationship, you will have to assume and speak as though you actually do have the God-given, constitutional, and economic right to connect directly with VITO, establish and maintain Equal Business Stature, learn about VITO's interests and objectives, share an idea or two, and see what happens.

You do have that right!

When you actually believe those five words you just read, you will be using the same "headset" – the same positive, results-oriented, cut-to-the-chase way of looking at the world – that VITO uses to connect with other VITOs!

It's much, much easier to do this than you may have been led to believe. And the key to *making* it easy lies in focusing on HOW VITO SELLS. Don't get distracted by anything that has no bearing whatsoever on VITO's purchasing decisions – like, for instance, the title that's been printed on your business card. Ask yourself: How does VITO buy?

In the chapters that follow, you're going to focus like a laser beam on HOW VITO SELLS. There's a very important reason for that: As it happens, VITOs *buy* in precisely the same way they *sell.* So: If you know their selling process…you will know how they want to buy from you. And you know what? VITOs actually *love* to deal with people who use Equal Business Stature intelligently…people who mirror their **attitudes** and **behaviors,** and mirror their processes, to help them buy the results they really *want* to buy.

Truth be told, VITOs love to buy. But they hate to be "sold to" – at least, they hate to be "sold to" in the way that most salespeople consider themselves to be "selling."

As it happens, you have to sell to VITO using *VITO's process,* on *VITO's terms.* That means you have to understand what *they* do when *they* establish Equal Business Stature. Before you go on, do the Action Step that follows on the next page.

ACTION STEP

Think of a specific prospective customer or an existing customer account. In the space below, briefly describe your own understanding of how VITOs in that industry sells to other VITOs. What do you think they do when they want to drive the sales process forward?

CHAPTER SIX

"People buy emotionally; they make decisions intellectually." – David Sandler

VITO's Selling (and Buying!) Process: Bonding and Rapport

More often than not, VITO will reach out to other VITOs in order to win new customers for their organizations. Whether they consciously realize that it's what they're doing or not, VITOs who sell this way invariably follow a predictable five-step process for qualifying and closing selling opportunities. The five-step process they follow intuitively, perhaps without quite being able to describe what they're doing, is the same one Sandler Training has formalized and taught to salespeople in virtually all industries.

The first three steps of the process represent the *Qualifying* phase of the selling process. The final two steps represent the *Closing* phase of the process.

Naturally, not all the VITOs that VITO reaches out to will make it past the first three *Qualifying* steps. In fact, a prospect can be disqualified at any step in the process. But the point we want you to bear in mind here is that, whenever VITO sells, VITO always sells *in a specific five-step sequence.* That sequence looks like this: **Pain, Budget, Decision, Fulfillment,** and **Post-Sell.**

So what are we saying? Specifically, we're saying that, once the sales discussion has begun in earnest, VITO will address everything that has to happen in that first step, Pain, and lock that step down tight, *before* moving on to the next step. The five steps constitute the Sandler Selling System.

The whole model, in fact, fits into something known as the Sandler Submarine. The Submarine was created by Sandler Selling System founder David Sandler. Here's how he described it in his book *You Can't Teach a Kid to Ride a Bicycle at a Seminar* (Dutton, 1995).

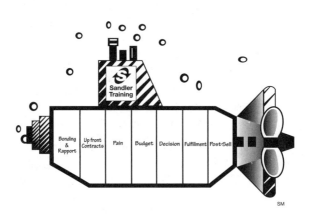

Look at the submarine in the illustration above. Remember the World War II movies in which a depth charge hits dangerously close to the stern of the submarine? The hero rushes below deck, summons the men out of the damaged compartment, slams the thick metal door, and spins the wheel as the compartment fills with water. There's no way to get back into that compartment, but the ship stays afloat. Tensions mount, the film rolls on, and the next compartment begins to fill with water. Again, the hero mves the men forward, slams the thick metal door, spins the wheel, and the compartment fills with water. And so the process continues until each compartment fills with water, and the men continue moving forward to safety and to success.

This submarine story is an excellent analogy for the Sandler Selling System. Take a look for yourself. You'll notice that each compartment of the submarine represents a step in the Sandler selling process. What happens when you use the system? Of course: You advance your prospect, step by step, toward a successful sale – because you finish the work in one compartment and then close it. You don't go "backwards" and neither does your prospect.

As you looked at Mr. Sandler's submarine, you may have noticed that two compartments, Bonding and Rapport, and Up-Front Contracts, come to the left of the other five steps we just shared with you. That's because VITOs – and all effective salespeople – use these two elements at the beginning of the relationship to launch the whole process. That's not all they do, though. In fact, if you're going to model VITO's approach to selling, you will use Bonding and Rapport and Up-Front Contracts throughout the sales discussion and the relationship. As you will see, these two elements incorporate concepts, methods, and actions that support the entire sales process -- and in fact make it possible for you to move from one compartment to the next.

To put it bluntly, if you lose your early rapport with the prospect, or do something to destroy the bond you've built up on a promising first call, you can't realistically expect to make it through the five steps that follow and close the deal.

By the same token, if you don't get good up-front contracts from your prospects at *each* key stage of the discussion, you won't really be in control of the process. (We'll share more on what an Up-Front Contract is in the next chapter.) By the way: Can you guess who's in control of any sales process VITO initiates? You've got it: VITO. So whose example are you going to follow when it comes to securing commitments about *what happens next?* Of course: VITO's.

Let's take just a moment to look more closely at how the critical idea of bonding and rapport fits into VITO's selling process. For VITO to communicate effectively with any prospect, there has to be some rapport between them, and that's typically going to be based on something VITO says to *put the prospect at ease and send the unspoken message that "everything's okay" in the prospect's world and in VITO's world.* This sense of "okay-ness" helps to create and sustain a comfortable environment in which to do business, and making sure that environment exists is part of VITO's job when he reaches out to another VITO. That responsibility starts the minute VITO says, "Hello," and, of course, continues throughout the relationship. Specifically, VITO uses the power of personality, and perhaps some humor, to get the conversation "on track" and positive.

That's bonding and rapport: the first compartment. Again, the job of establishing bonding and rapport really doesn't *stop* at any point in the selling process...but VITO's selling process really can't *start* without it.

Bonding and Rapport – by means of listening and noticing body language – is a huge part of how VITO sells. You're going to use exactly the same strategy to make sure VITO is comfortable *buying* from you.

CHAPTER SEVEN

"Inspect what you expect."
– David Sandler

VITO's Selling (and Buying!) Process: Up-Front Contracts

The term *Up-Front Contracts* refers to a process for maintaining control of the discussion, adding predictability to the selling process, and making sure that VITO and the prospect are really "on the same page." To understand this concept, all you have to do is ask yourself this question: *Would VITO ever invest VITO, Inc.'s time, money, and human resources in any process WITHOUT knowing what was going to happen as a result of that investment?*

No way. VITO makes investments only when VITO knows *exactly* what's going to happen next. And that's the philosophy you're going to adopt as well, when you reach out to VITO.

To avoid disappointment, frustration, and unfulfilled expectations, VITO establishes clear agreements ahead of time about exactly what will happen in advance of each new discussion about an opportunity that will benefit both sides. Phone calls or meetings don't end with VITO agreeing to vague or nonexistent "commitments" like "Go spend three weeks working on a proposal, and then we'll think about it and let you know." VITO makes sure that both sides are engaged, involved, and invested in the intended outcome of the next sales encounter.

Most selling situations require more than one meeting or phone call. As a result, VITO (and, indeed, all truly superior salespeople) establish clear objectives for *each* meeting, clear understandings of the role each party will play in reaching the objectives, clear time allotments, and so on. Notice that VITO is careful to establish these contracts *prior* to any upcoming discussion.

Think of it this way. Any time two VITOs have an ongoing series of discussions about a mutual opportunity, *each VITO will get very, very clear* about exactly what is happening next, when it's happening, and who's responsible for making it happen. That clarity will be evident before the call concludes.

This idea of an up-front contract not only adds predictability to the meeting, but also becomes the benchmark by which VITO – or anyone else – can easily measure the productivity of the meeting. Notice again that up-front contracts are definitely an *early and important* part of the selling process…but, like the bonding and rapport concept, they are simply how VITO does business. In later chapters, we'll give you specific examples of how VITO negotiates up-front contracts and thus maintains control of the sales process.

Winning up-front contracts – by means of setting clear benchmarks and expectations for both sides about exactly "what happens next" and when – is a huge part of how VITO sells. You're going to use exactly the same strategy to make sure VITO is comfortable *buying* from you.

CHAPTER EIGHT

"It is PAIN that will get you the sale – not price."
– David Sandler

VITO's Selling (and Buying!) Process: Pain

When top officers sell to other top officers, they usually end up implementing (whether they realize it or not) the Sandler concept of Pain. This means simply that they identify a *problem* or situation for which the prospect is looking for a remedy…they identify the underlying *reasons* for the problem…and they then get clear on the *impact* the problem has, or is likely to have, in the prospect's world.

Think of Pain as a three-piece jigsaw puzzle. One piece represents the *problem* situation itself. Another piece represents the various *reasons* for the problem. And the final piece represents the *impact* of the problem. VITOs are, in general, experts at discussing all three pieces of the puzzle, especially with other VITOs. That's how they sell.

The objective of this step in the Sandler Selling System is simply to work collaboratively with the other person to fit the puzzle pieces together and get a clear picture of what's happening. In an effective sales conversation, the three all fit together as part of a seamless whole that can be remedied by the top officer's product or service. If the pain *cannot* be remedied by anything VITO, Inc. does, VITO moves on. The prospect has been disqualified, and is no longer on VITO's priority list.

Recognizing problem situations, identifying the reasons for them, and establishing the true impact they have on people and organizations is an art, one that most VITOs have mastered from long practice. In later chapters of this book, we'll share some of their most powerful Pain strategies with you.

Identifying the Pain – by getting clear on the gaps between what a prospect expects and what is actually happening, the cause of those gaps, and the real-world impact of those gaps – is a huge part of how VITO sells. You're going to use exactly the same strategy to make sure VITO is comfortable *buying* from you.

CHAPTER NINE

"You must determine whether
your prospect has the necessary funds available
to purchase your product or service."
– David Sandler

VITO's Selling (and Buying!) Process: Budget

In completing the Budget step, the top officer, consciously or unconsciously, is following the part of the Sandler sequence that confirms beyond a shadow of a doubt, that a given prospect is *qualified* to invest resources. At this stage, we determine that the prospect is both willing and able to commit the resources necessary to buy from us and work with us. *VITO* simply won't make the investment of significant amounts of time and energy with anyone else.

When we use the term "investment," we may be referring to money but we may also be talking about a time investment or even an investment in a change in the way an organization operates. If there is both the willingness and the ability to make an investment, VITO will conclude that it makes sense to move on to the next steps of the relationship. That means VITO identifies, for certain, whether the prospect has funding that can be devoted to the purchase; whether the prospect has previously purchased similar products and services and if so, what the investment actually was and what payback resulted; and what the prospect's current expectations from the investment are.

By the way: When VITOs want to make sure they are getting straight answers on these questions, who are they going to ask? You've got it:

another VITO!

VITOs don't beat around the bush when it comes to getting a realistic idea of what the prospect's investment in their products or services really is (or isn't) likely to be. They use effective communication techniques to get prospects to share meaningful information that lets them figure out exactly what kind of opportunity they're looking at. We'll share some of those strategies with you in later chapters. For now, understand that getting clarity, sooner rather than later, about Budget is a huge part of how VITO sells. You're going to use exactly the same strategy to make sure VITO is comfortable *buying* from you.

CHAPTER TEN

"Find out the who, where, when, why, and how."
– David Sandler

VITO's Selling (and Buying!) Process: Decision

The Decision step of the Sandler Selling System is the final *Qualifying* step. It's where VITO – and every other truly effective salesperson – finds out what the prospect's process is going to be for making a buying decision.

As top officers move through the Pain, Budget, and Decision steps of the relationship, they are constantly evaluating the opportunity in order to figure out whether it meets their criteria for a "qualified" prospect. When they commit to the selling process, they invariably figure out what those buying criteria are *before* delivering a presentation – and, in fact, they are likely to build those criteria into the presentation! If they can't identify what the decision making process is, how the organization's structure has delivered buying decisions in the past, when the final decision is to be made, how the timing will eventually affect fulfillment, who is to make the decision, and *why* decisions are made that way, they will not deliver the presentation.

Unless and until top officers have figured all of that out, they know that they are not ready to proceed with a presentation. If the prospect cannot identify the actual requirements of the decision making process, the opportunity is disqualified.

We've come face-to-face, once again, with a critical competitive advantage that people who sell to VITOs have over all other sellers. In order to answer all those questions about the decision making process, we are probably going to need *access to players across the enterprise.* Who is the only person we can expect to *give* us that access? It's VITO, of course! And this, obviously, is one of the big reasons VITOs invariably start by reaching out to *other* VITOs when it's time to add new logos to their customer list. They want to "cut to the chase" – that is, figure out exactly what the real decision making criteria are going to be – and they know that other VITOs will respect their need for that information.

Understanding exactly how and why buying decisions have been made in the past, as well as how and why they are going to be made now, is a huge part of how VITO sells. You're going to use exactly the same strategy to make sure VITO is comfortable *buying* from you.

CHAPTER ELEVEN

"Close the sale or close the prospect's file."
– David Sandler

VITO's Selling (and Buying!) Process: Fulfillment

The Fulfillment step of the Sandler Selling System is the outcome of successfully completing the Pain, Budget, and Decision steps – and winning the prospect's commitment to view your presentation and make a decision based on that commitment.

The most effective sales professionals – and VITOs are nothing if not effective salespeople – invariably deliver this commitment-based presentation as the *culmination* of all the work that has gone before. They don't add new bells and whistles or throw in new variables that are likely to clutter up the decision making process. They address the elements of the prospect's situation that were uncovered in the Pain step – nothing more and nothing less.

Top officers know – and you should know – that the goal here is a simple, straightforward one: to get an up-or-down decision – not to land the sale in the "no-man's land" of "we'll think about it." Typically, the top officer's presentation to a fellow top officer is *predicated* on a commitment to make a decision on the spot, at the conclusion of the meeting. If something has changed that alters the qualification of the opportunity or the prospect's ability or willingness to make a decision, the presentation may have to be rescheduled or cancelled.

These days, presentations from VITOs can take many forms. In later chapters of this book, we'll share the best VITO strategies for closing the deal and moving forward with the relationship – whether the confirmation is supposed to come in person, over the phone, or via some other communication medium.

Executing the Fulfillment step – by delivering a commitment-based presentation that builds on all the mutual work that has gone before – is a huge part of how VITO sells. You're going to use exactly the same strategy to make sure VITO is comfortable *buying* from you.

CHAPTER TWELVE

"Don't buy back tomorrow the product or service you sold today." – David Sandler

VITO's Selling (and Buying!) Process: Post-Sell

The Post-Sell step of the Sander Selling System is another step where most top officers intuitively follow the process that delivers sales excellence. In doing so, they act on two complementary goals. First, they lock up the sale. And second, they facilitate the transition of the relationship from that of buyer-seller to that of customer-provider.

It's not unusual for prospects to have second thoughts after making a positive buying decision. They wonder, "Did I make the right decision?" "Am I paying too much?" "Will the company deliver as promised?" VITOs – and all effective sellers – know that unless those unasked questions are addressed, the prospect will be tempted to back out of the decision.

That's why VITOs invariably begin the Post-Sell step immediately *after* the purchase decision. During this step, they will ask questions like:

- Are you 100% comfortable with your decision?
- Is there anything we need to revisit before we sign the agreement?
- Is there anything we didn't cover that might give you reason to have second thoughts?
- If there were one thing that would cause you to put the order on hold or cancel it, what would that be?

In later chapters of the book, we'll give you more examples of the various techniques VITOs use to execute the Post-Sell step in a powerful and compelling way. For now, though, understand this: Bringing up potential roadblocks to the relationship – as opposed to avoiding them – is a huge part of VITO's strategy for formalizing the "yes" decision and avoiding buyer's remorse. You're going to use exactly the same strategy to make sure VITO is comfortable *buying* from you... and staying with you.

PART TWO:
SET...

CHAPTER THIRTEEEN

"Develop a prospecting awareness." – David Sandler

Your Real Job Description

Now you know.

You know for sure that you have a whole lot in common with VITO, the Approver of your sale – more in common with VITO, in fact, than with anyone else in the organization. You also know exactly how VITOs sell.

Now let's put those two pieces of information together.

We firmly believe that there's actually *one and only one* reason that you're in the sales business at all, and that's to **take advantage of your commonalities with VITO and make sure you connect, on a regular basis, with as many VITOs as you can – in a way that matches up with their own selling style.**

That little gem is worth repeating to yourself a couple of times.

Here's another way to look at the same career-changing idea: VITO will buy in exactly the way VITO sells. And your job is simply to model VITO's selling process back at as many VITOs as possible. That's what you should be doing for a living.

Once you connect up with VITO and get really, really good at having conversations that actually match up with VITO's own selling process, you will, by definition, have found VITO's buying process! Your task then becomes a fairly simple one: Use your organization's resources to satisfy VITO's requirements and exceed VITO's expectations.

But the good connection with VITO must come first. That's your job: Making good connections with VITO! And note that we're using the word "good" to mean "effective, by VITO's own standards, in moving the sale forward."

It doesn't matter what it says in your job description or on your business card. It doesn't matter what your spouse tells people you do for a living. It doesn't matter what your parents tell people you do for a living. It doesn't matter what the IRS thinks you do for a living. In our view, what you really should be doing for a living is making good connections with VITO. In fact, if you're doing anything else, there's a problem.

Your job as a top salesperson has nothing to do with your product's feature set, or the speed of your widgets, or the number of times your organization has won awards for engineering or service or public relations excellence, or the popularity of your brand. That's all interesting, and it's all potentially important, but it's not what you do to earn your paycheck…because it's not what VITO buys!

Your job is simply to reach out to large numbers of VITOs and have effective sales conversations – conversations that mirror VITO's own selling process. Specifically, your job is to execute, with due diligence, those crucial first five minutes – the five minutes that will very likely determine the course the entire relationship will follow.

How exactly will you do that? Well in very broad terms, you already know. You're going to reach out to VITO in exactly the way VITO would reach out to other high-level Approvers…by working your way through this (familiar) sequence:

- **Bonding and Rapport**
- **Up-Front Contract**
- **Pain**
- **Budget**
- **Decision**
- **Fulfillment**
- **Post-Sell**

We'll give you examples and strategies for all of this. Just remember, please, the pervasive nature of the first two elements. You will need to build and sustain rapport every step of the way with VITO. And then, after having built rapport, you will never, ever forget that VITO doesn't do anything without knowing exactly what's going to happen next. And guess what? You won't do anything without knowing what's going to happen next, either!

You'll be requesting an up-front contract confidently, as someone who has Equal Business Stature with VITO. In short, you're going to be asking for commitments, just like VITO does, before you invest your own time and energy or your organization's resources.

And that's really the point we want you to take away from this chapter: **When VITO sells, VITO lives and asks for commitments – so if you're going to play in VITO's world, you must live by commitments and learn to ask for commitments, as well.**

That's the biggest part of your job! You must learn how and when to win those commitments. You must learn when to ask for little ones, when to ask for big ones, and exactly what you should do when you don't get them. But first you must get clear on the fact that it's asking *VITO first* for those commitments – not the Decision Maker, not the Influencer, not the Recommender – that will *earn you commissions.*

Securing up-front contracts with VITO before you invest significant time and energy in the relationship is not a one-time event. It's a way of life, the only way of life that VITO respects. If you really want to earn five good minutes with VITO, you must be willing to earn that respect. Asking for up-front contracts is thus going to be a consistent element of your relationship with VITO, just like bonding and rapport is. (We're emphasizing the up-front contracts here, though, because most salespeople are already pretty good at the bonding and rapport skill.)

From this point forward in the book, you'll be getting a whole lot of tools that are designed especially to help you accelerate the bonding and rapport process – not only with VITO, but with VITO's trusted advisor and Personal Assistant, Tommie, who's a critical player in VITO's world, and thus in yours.

CHAPTER FOURTEEN

"Need to excel." – David Sandler

Some Definitions, Some Answers

Let's get down to business.

We've already identified the four different categories of individuals you're most likely to run into within VITO, Inc. Now, let's categorize the organizations within your sales territory.

Suspects are organizations that you have reasons to believe would make great customers, but who have not contacted you and whom you have not yet contacted.

Prospects are organizations that you have made contact with (or that contacted you). You're currently and actively attempting to get them to buy from you.

Customers are organizations that have invested in your products, services, and solutions and are still using what you sold them, but are not currently buying from you.

Existing Customers are individuals or organizations that currently buy from you. The operative word here is currently. These are not people who bought from you once upon a time. These are not people who you believe are going to buy from you in the future. These are people who, at this moment, are continuing to invest in your products, services and solutions. In other words, they are presently helping you meet your quota.

VIP Customers are organizations that fit the definition of an Existing Customer and are willing give you all of the following:

- "Golden referrals."
- Priceless testimonials.
- Valuable add-on business.
- Uncensored access to individuals and departments across and up the enterprise.
- Opportunities that go far beyond your immediate business relationship.

Your job now – and it's a vitally important one – is to uncover and fully define the *reasons* you currently have Existing Customers and VIP customers. The answers you come up with will point you like a laser-beam in the precise direction of **VITO suspects and prospects who are pre-disposed to buy from you.** Is this worth knowing? Absolutely. Is this worth spending a few minutes out of your busy day on? That's up to you. Remember, you and you alone are accountable for the results you get from this program.

What follows is critically important to your sales career. Find a quiet place. Close the door. Turn off the phones, put your Blackberry® down. For the next twenty to thirty minutes, give the four Action Steps on the following pages your undivided attention.

"No pain, no sell." – David Sandler

ACTION STEP #1

What would happen at your very best Existing or VIP Customer's operation if your product, service, or solution were to mysteriously disappear? What would happen to this organization's day-to-day operation? How would not having what they invested in affect their shareholder value, margins, ability to generate revenue, contain costs, deliver their products, maintain compliance, satisfy their customers, and maintain their brand's image in the marketplace? In other words, how would not having the results and benefits of what you've sold them hurt their top, middle, and bottom line? Write your answer below.

ACTION STEP #2

Take a look at your current "book of business" and select your very best VIP Customer(s). You know, the one(s) that you really love to visit with...the one(s) who were an instant, natural fit for what you have to offer, and who connected with you quickly and easily...the one(s) who are the easiest for you to work with. Got it? (If you are still drawing a blank because you just got this job, talk to your sales manager and pick someone else's VIP Customer.) What is this (are these) industry(ies), and who is (are) your primary contact(s) there? Write your answers below.

ACTION STEP #3

List the Hard value you've delivered for that VIP Customer(s). Hard value is measurable - you can express it in numbers or percentages. For example, has your business relationship with this organization delivered greater revenues by "X" percent? Has the relationship quantifiably improved efficiencies in any department by "X" percent? Has the relationship created any quantifiable reduction in expenses by "X" dollars? Has the relationship compressed time-to-market by a measurable amount of days, weeks or months? Has the relationship helped your VIP Customer(s) reach full compliance within a mere "X" days, weeks or months? Sometimes it's easier to quantify the Hard value if you think again about that mysterious, hypothetical disappearance of your stuff that happened in the dark of the night. How would you measure the negative impact such a loss would have in the overall operation? Write your answers below.

ACTION STEP #4

Now list the Soft value you've delivered to your VIP Customer(s). This is more difficult to measure because this time around, you aren't expressing the values as numbers or percentages. You'll be articulating Soft value using descriptive words and phrases like these: "Greater peace of mind." "Less risk and worry." "Mitigation of risk." "Substantial savings or cost control." "Greater concentration on core business initiatives." "Enhanced brand recognition." "Improved image in the marketplace." Write some examples of Soft value you've actually delivered for your VIP Customer(s) in the space below.

Yeah, yeah – we know – it looks like a lot of work.

But is your **Five Minutes with VITO** worth it? You bet. Anyway, you should know that nothing that follows in this book will make much sense if you don't write down real answers in all the previous action steps. (If you want, you can use a separate sheet of paper.)

You're halfway home! In the next chapter, we'll use the information you just developed to get a handle on something called the **Consequence of Not Taking Action**…which is a critical point of interest for each and every VITO you encounter. Keep going!

CHAPTER FIFTEEN

"When the prospect is neutral, get him moving."
– David Sandler

Establishing the Consequences of Not Taking Action

One of the critical strategies you will use to **build rapport** and **establish up-front contracts** with VITO during your critical five-minute "window" appeals to something all VITOs, *by definition*, hate: it's anything that looks, smells, or feels like inaction.

VITOs *loathe* doing nothing, and will do just about anything to avoid people and things that are inactive. This is a rule of business life that only a tiny minority of salespeople have learned to take advantage of. You're about to take advantage of it, though, and you're going to do so by means of this easy-to-remember, and *extremely reliable* standard:

- If you're talking to someone whose basic approach to business (and life in general) consists of finding reasons not to take action, someone who *hates* to make the decisions that make new action possible...then you are *not talking to VITO*.

- On the other hand, if you're talking to someone who instinctively *loves* taking action, someone who *relishes* launching the choices that start whole new lines of action ricocheting throughout the organization...you're *probably talking to VITO*.

VITO is so in love with the idea of taking action and making decisions that the sheer volume of decisions and actions sometimes drives the other players in VITO's world to distraction. (These folks generally keep their frustration to themselves, of course.) Very often, there are so many brand-new decisions from VITO's office, so many brand-new lines of action playing out as a result of casual five-minute conversations with VITO, that it's sometimes hard to tell what really is "top priority" at any given moment at VITO, Inc.

The top priorities *seem* to keep changing...but you'll notice they change in a way that consistently supports VITO's goals, dreams, and aspirations for the organization.

As it happens, there's a very simple reason for the tidal wave of decisions and action items that roar out of VITO's office every working day. The reason is this: *One of the biggest "sins" in VITO's world is failing to take the necessary action to turn VITO's goals, dreams, and aspirations into reality.*

You're going to put that principle to work for your own sales process...by identifying the *cost* of inaction in an area that connects to your product, service, or solution.

Take a moment for yourself when you finish reading this paragraph – a moment just to *THINK*. Go back to the work you did in Chapter Fourteen. Review it closely. Think about *exactly what VITO stands to lose* – that your VIP customers definitely *would* lose – if your product, service, or solution pulled a disappearing act. In other words: What disaster do you prevent or miracle do you make possible? How could you back up your claim to be able to prevent that disaster or deliver that miracle with substantial and substantiated appeals to both Hard and Soft value? How many jet engines would ship safely to new customers, and not go skidding across the factory floor, over the course of say, a year? By how much could you reduce the time it takes one of your new customers to bring a product to market? What would the improvements in a new customer's key relationships with customers, vendors, and employees feel like to that customer? Take just a moment to *THINK* about those and similar questions right now, by reviewing your written work at the end of Chapter Fourteen. We'll wait right here for you.

Welcome back. It's time to sharpen your pencil again. Right now, you're going to be using the work you just reviewed in the last chapter to create a compelling, concisely stated idea that's capable of making VITO stop and wonder, "Okay – how the heck did they pull that off?"

To create that kind of idea, though, you're going to have to pull out different pieces of what you did in Chapter Fourteen and polish them up, step by step. Don't worry. It's going to be painless. We're going to show you exactly what the recipe is for this idea…the kind of idea that makes VITO wonder, "Wow. What happens if I *don't* take action?"

Fasten your seat belt, because we're going to build this VITO-specific, action-inspiring message with you, starting *now.* Let's get started!

First and foremost, we want you to get very clear on exactly what is the Hard value you deliver. This concept should be pretty clear to you by now, but take a look at the example that appears below. *Notice that there is no discussion whatsoever of your product's feature set in the statement you're about to read!*

> *Hard value: (THE MEASURABLE BENEFIT TO MY VIP CUSTOMER WAS THAT WE…) Improved efficiency of knowledge-based workers by up to 2.8%…(AND WE DID THIS BY MEANS OF A UNIQUE PROCESS THAT ALLOWED THEM TO…) get those knowledge workers spending more time analyzing and making decisions and less time gathering the information necessary to facilitate those decisions.*

Take note once again, please, that we're carefully identifying benefits and advantages, and *skipping the features and functions!* For the purposes of this exercise, we simply don't care how much or little the product or service weighs, costs, reconfigures, or was originally designed – and we certainly don't care how many lines of programming code it now incorporates or the names of the special materials used to build it. *That's not VITO-SPEAK!*

Write your own *Hard value bullet* in the space below, using the text in the box above as a model. Base your Hard value bullet on the work you did at the conclusion of Chapter Fourteen. If you didn't do that work, go back and finish it now, and then come back and fill in this space.

Hard value: (THE MEASURABLE BENEFIT TO MY VIP CUSTOMER WAS THAT WE...)

(AND WE DELIVERED THIS BY MEANS OF A UNIQUE PROCESS THAT ALLOWED THEM TO...)

Benefits first – advantages second. Get it?

Now you're going to create a *Soft value bullet* along identical lines. Consider the example below, and notice once again that it does *not* appeal to the product or service feature set, and indeed avoids even referencing the features!

> ***Soft value: (THE UNMEASURABLE BENEFIT TO MY VIP CUSTOMER WAS THAT WE...) protected valuable market share and sustained their competitive edge...(AND WE DELIVERED THIS BY MEANS OF A UNIQUE PROCESS THAT ALLOWED THEM TO...) proactively identify and respond to competitor price moves and promotional offers – without lowering price points.***

Benefit first...advantage second...and *no feature or function dumps*. See the sequence?

Now create your own version. Write your own Soft value bullet in the space below, using the text in the box above as a model. Base your Soft value bullet on the work you did in the previous chapter. If that work still needs polishing, go back and polish it now, so you can complete this exercise.

(THE UNMEASURABLE BENEFIT TO MY VIP CUSTOMER WAS THAT WE...)

(AND WE DELIVERED THIS BY MEANS OF A UNIQUE PROCESS THAT ALLOWED THEM TO...)

WARNING: It is impossible for you to take advantage of VITO's fear and hatred of inaction during your sales process if you do not complete the two written activities in this chapter! So do that.

See if you don't think it's all worth it. Once you've got good first drafts of your Hard value bullets and Soft value bullets, you'll blow your own mind in Chapter Sixteen by creating a single sentence capable of delivering real-world results like this one:

Tony:

"I did exactly what you told me to do. Highlighted certain elements of my correspondence. I am ecstatic! VITO took my call, I landed the appointment and the largest sale in the history of my company. It all happened so fast I thought I was dreaming. Thank you, thank you, thank you!"

Nance R.
Chicago, Ill.

To turn the work you've done thus far into the kind of idea that Nance actually used to **build rapport** and **up-front contracts** with VITO, you will need to understand a simple, but critical, principle of the specialized language we call *VITO-SPEAK*. That principle is called the *Balanced Gain Equation*, and we'll tell you what it is and how to use it in the next chapter. But first, complete the Action Step on the next page.

ACTION STEP

What would happen to VITO's business if two straight months went by without VITO, Inc. experiencing ANY of the Hard or Soft value that you deliver? Be as specific as you can. Write your answer in the space below.

CHAPTER SIXTEEN

"Express your feelings through third-party stories."
– David Sandler

The Balanced Gain Equation

VITO, like everyone else on earth, is motivated by two powerful, galvanizing possibilities. Possible Motivation Number One is the chance of experiencing pleasure or reward. Possible Motivation Number Two is the chance to avoid doom, demise, disaster, and failure (i.e., avoid pain).

On the large scale, that's really all there is in terms of motivation. VITO is either going to try to move toward a positive experience (for instance, making money or increasing internal efficiency) or away from a negative experience (for instance, budget overruns, eroding market-share and/or shareholder confidence, or even the prospect of landing in jail because VITO, Inc. was not in compliance with some arcane government regulation).

The motivations that actually drive VITO then, fall into the same two broad categories that everyone else's motivations fall into. What's different is what happens when VITO balances those motivations to decide which initiative should get the "green light" in any given situation. That balancing act happens differently with VITO than it does with anyone else at VITO, Inc., and for a very good reason. **No one else at VITO, Inc. is responsible for the stuff that VITO is ultimately responsible for – namely, everything.**

Understand: VITOs are "whole brain" thinkers who are constantly on the lookout for other "whole brain" thinkers who can serve as their allies, confidants, thought partners and key suppliers.

What do we mean by that? We mean that VITOs are paid to look at both the potential up-side and the potential downside of each and every business opportunity. That's how they balance their own motivations, the world at large, and indeed, every single one of the options placed before them at any given moment. If you start taking this same "whole brain" approach to the vexing issues that confront VITO, and consistently communicate about them in the same way VITO does, *you will eventually become an ally*. That's a promise. On the other hand, if you take the "partial brain" approach that drives ninety-eight out of a hundred people who interact with VITO over the course of the day, and if you communicate about those same problems in the way that most people communicate about them, *you will not become an ally of VITO*.

So, for instance, if we're beginning a conversation with VITO and we speak aggressively and passionately about the goal of "increasing consumer awareness of VITO, Inc.'s in the marketplace," we can expect VITO to do a mental double-check about the possible *pain*, as well as the possible *pleasure*, that could arise from such an initiative.

Are you with us so far? Good. Watch where this road goes, as it's incredibly important to your journey.

We can expect VITO to run that pain-and-pleasure check through what we call *VITOpedia* which is essentially VITO's encyclopedic understanding of pretty much *everything that has ever happened in every nook and cranny of VITO, Inc.* Think for just a moment about what that really means to your sale, and to your possible relationship with VITO. What could go wrong when VITO starts asking him or herself, "What could go wrong?"

Look at it again. When we start holding forth about what a wonderful idea it's going to be to "increase consumer awareness of VITO, Inc. in the marketplace," we can generally expect VITO to say (or, in the worst-case scenario, merely think) something like this: "What a load of baloney. Heck, I could "increase our awareness" among consumers tomorrow morning – all I'd have to do is quadruple our advertising budget. The question is, if I did that, would

I be winning consumers awareness in a *cost-effective way that actually supports the overachievement of our marketing goals?"*

Can you see the problem with only talking about a single dimension of a complex issue? When VITO makes a decision, VITO can't just think of how it affects one corner of the organization. Unlike everyone else in the building, VITO has to think of how the decision he or she is about to make will affect *every square inch* of VITO, Inc.

Fact #1: Just about every business opportunity that you will ever present to VITO will have some element of possible *opportunities for pleasure or reward* associated with it.

Fact #2: Just about every business opportunity that you will ever present to VITO will have some element of *avoiding pain or disaster* associated with it.

The trick is *balancing* those motivators in a way that takes into account VITO's unique, real-world responsibility to make decisions that advance the interests, not just of the sales department or the accounting department, but of the enterprise as a whole.

Therefore, whenever we communicate with VITO, whether we do so by means of written correspondence, verbal communication, or electronic communication of some sort, we will communicate with what we'll choose to call a Balanced Gain Equation – a clear signal to VITO that we, too, have thought about all the possible upsides and all the possible downsides. We will let VITO know that we have identified and compensated for the (inevitable) problems or hurdles that any successful initiative must identify and overcome. So…instead of simply talking about "increasing consumer awareness of VITO, Inc.'s position in the marketplace" – which is, we promise you, a bad discussion waiting to happen – we're instead going to talk to VITO about a Big Idea like this one:

Based on experience dealing with marketing initiatives in your industry...

...we believe we could increase targeted consumer awareness of VITO, Inc.'s products by as much as 30%...

...while REDUCING marketing costs.

What a difference! In this example, we've made it clear to VITO that the program we're considering, the kind of solution that we *may* be able to deliver, has to get past the same multi-dimensional obstacles that VITO has to get past each and every day. This isn't just an excuse to burn up some dollars in the marketing budget. It's part of the strategic plan for cost containment...*that increases public awareness of VITO, Inc.!* Suddenly, VITO wants to know more!

Yes, building a Balanced Gain Equation for a specific VITO takes time and thought and care. And yes, turning VITO off by promising the moon takes no time and very little thought or care. *Your five great minutes with VITO will definitely be worth the investment!*

One More Thing...

There's actually a little bit more to what has to go into the Balanced Gain Equation if it is to stop VITO in his or her tracks... and get VITO to start thinking seriously about the costs of *not* taking action.

Any time we create a Balanced Gain Equation that reflects what we *think, suspect,* or *are curious about* that we might be able to do for VITO, we must be careful to include the element of time. This is because VITO lives in a time-compressed world (as, indeed you do and all effective salespeople do). Just about everything in VITO's business life connects to deadlines, schedules, and projected completion dates. VITOs know, better than anyone else in the organization, what "ripple effects" play out at VITO, Inc. when goals, plans and objectives fall behind schedule. Usually, VITO's new product releases live and, alas, die based on how they stack up against the calendar. So if we truly want to get VITO's attention and interest, our "equation" is not complete until it features some reference to time.

Take a look:

Based on experience dealing with marketing initiatives in your industry...

...we suspect we could increase targeted consumer awareness of VITO, Inc.'s products by as much as 30%...

...while REDUCING marketing costs...

...within the next 90 days.

Understand – this is not a "script" that you're going to recite to VITO, but rather a *blueprint for a powerful idea* that you can use to build rapport during those first critical moments when you interact with VITO.

Before you go any further, why not try your hand at taking the good work you did on the Hard value and Soft value bullet points in the last chapter...and transform those bullets it into a Balanced Gain Equation similar to the one you just read?

Don't worry about getting it perfect on the first try. We're going to be coming back to this again. In fact, *creating this Big Idea is the real objective of Part Two of this book,* so you should prepare yourself right now to take full advantage of the combined decades of expertise we're offering you here and make the very most of this opportunity to hone and fine-tune this critical tactic in your initial approach to VITO.

"Product knowledge used at the wrong time can be intimidating." – David Sandler

Complete the Action Step below – then move on to Chapter Seventeen.

ACTION STEP

Using the Hard value and Soft value bullets created in the previous chapter, build a Balanced Gain Equation that incorporates the element of time, just like the example you saw in this chapter. It doesn't have to be perfect. We'll be sharing more examples of Balanced Gain Equations in future pages and helping you to fine tune what you come up with here. But you must create a short draft now based on the work you've done up to this point!

CHAPTER SEVENTEEN

"No mutual mystification." – David Sandler

Close-up on the Big Idea

VITO, Inc. lives or dies according to the success or failure of the Big Ideas that pass VITO's "whole-brain" Balanced Gain test.

That's worth reading again. So please read it a second time, right now. And when you're done reading it for the second time, try reading it out loud. After that, you might consider writing it in big letters and posting it in your cubicle, on your dashboard, or maybe even on the refrigerator next to the picture of the hot sports car, new penthouse, new closet, or trip around the world you are currently in the process of manifesting by reading and implementing the principles laid out in this book.

VITO, Inc. lives or dies on big ideas. And the only Big Ideas that ever get implemented at VITO, Inc. are the ones that pass VITO's "whole brain" test.

What is a Big Idea? Put bluntly, it's a concisely, energetically stated initiative that can either make VITO money, save VITO money, improve a process at VITO, Inc., or keep VITO out of jail. That's the kind of initiative VITO can invest time in understanding and discussing, and either get behind personally or ask someone else to take on responsibility for evaluating. A Big Idea is something that stands out from the competing traffic on VITO's desk because it is perceived as having a realistic prospect of actually delivering a major win for VITO.

You have a *right* to share Big Ideas with VITO. Remember the "ten out of ten" level of Equal Business Stature you established in Part One? This is how that Equal Business Stature gets used in the real world...by sharing Big Ideas with VITO!

You have a *duty* to share Big Ideas with VITO. As we saw in Chapter Thirteen, it's part of your job description! Remember, your real job, no matter what anyone else thinks, is to interact with and communicate with VITO – in a way that matches VITO's own sales cycle. Can you guess *how* VITO executes that sales cycle when it's time for winning new customers? By reaching out to other VITOs and – you guessed it – sharing Big Ideas!

And here's the point you need to master now: Every single Big Idea you share with VITO, without exception, *must* take the form of a Balanced Gain Equation that incorporates the element of time, and points toward a *major win* for VITO. In fact, for our purposes, that's the only working definition for a Big Idea that's worth using. Why? Because sharing and refining *Big Ideas* so that they fit perfectly into VITO's world will help you...

- Establish bonding and rapport *by appealing to your Equal Business Stature with VITO.*
- Win up-front contracts *that allow both sides to conclude that it makes sense to move forward step by step to turn the Big Idea into reality.*
- Quantify pain *that is currently keeping VITO from overachieving on specific goals that connect to the Big Idea.*
- Clarify the dollars involved *because both you and VITO know that the investment and the deliverables must be understood by both sides if the Big Idea is to be implemented.*
- Get clear on the decision process *by clarifying the benchmarks you and VITO will be using to "pull the trigger" on the Big Idea.*
- Complete the Fulfillment step *and secure the formal commitment to the Big Idea.*
- Post-Sell *and lay the groundwork for a long-term relationship with VITO, based on your successful execution of the Big Idea.*

Yep – the Big Idea smoothes your way through the entire sales process. In fact, Big Ideas are so important that they are worth *constantly and endlessly improving.* You should be looking for ways to sharpen your Big Idea now, tomorrow, and forever, so that it matches up ever more precisely with a need in VITO's world. Your process of making the Big Idea you are hoping to share with VITO bigger, better, more concise, more compelling, and more closely tailored to VITO's world starts now. Create a template that seems likely to match up with the VITOs in a specific industry that you have not yet reached out to in your territory. Then get ready to refine that template, over and over again, based on new information. The process literally never ends!

Take a look now at how this process of constant and endless improvement plays out in real time.

Maybe you started out with this **BIG IDEA FOR VITO…**
"Increase new business revenue by as much as 15% while substantially containing a major element of your operational expenses within 90 days."

That's a good start! For one thing, it's only 22 words long. Anything over 35 words is dangerously long-winded by VITO's standards.

Notice that all the elements are present: the introduction of Hard value ("by as much as 15%") and Soft value in descriptive words ("substantially containing"), and the inclusion of the element of time ("within 90 days"). And it's balanced.

*But…*something about it feels vague and distant. This Big Idea, if committed to paper, is very likely to be placed on VITO's "gotta-read" pile. That means, in brutally practical terms, that it's never going to get read. You want to create something that inspires direct action *now,* either from VITO or from VITO's trusted assistant, Tommie. (That's because we want Tommie to highlight your Big Idea and put it under VITO's nose!). So – what can we do to take this version to the next level?

Maybe you tweak your Big Idea for ten or fifteen minutes and come up with this NEW Big Idea for VITO…

"Enhance shareholder value and dividends by increasing new business revenue by as much as 15% while containing a major element of your operational expenses – all within the next 90 days."

Notice that we've just introduced a major category of interest to VITO interest (shareholder value). By doing so, we've increased the odds of winning VITO's (or Tommie's) top-of-mind awareness. That's great! *But*…we still need to ask ourselves the question: What could we do to make it even better? What could we do to make VITO (or Tommie) drop everything else on a *very* busy day and say, "How on earth could they pull *that* off? We've got to call this person now."

Maybe you tweak your Big Idea for ten or fifteen minutes more and come up with yet another revision of your BIG IDEA FOR VITO:

"Five CEOs in your industry trust and rely on us to enhance shareholder value and dividends by increasing new business revenue by as much as 15% – while containing operational expenses. Time-to-value? 90 days."

Bingo! By introducing "social proof" ("Five CEOs in your industry trust and rely on us…") we have *locked in* a spot in VITO's (or Tommie's) immediate awareness. This is important. This matters. This is something worth investigating.

For now, don't worry about *how* this message will be getting to VITO or Tommie. (Fax? Phone call? E-mail? Carrier pigeon?) We'll cover all of that in Part Three. What you should be focusing on now is the *structure and key elements* of a *particular BIG IDEA FOR VITO* that you can refine down to 35 words or less. This BIG IDEA FOR VITO should focus on the goals and concerns of the VITOs in your territory in one particularly promising industry that you have *already sold to successfully*. (You can repeat the process later for VITOs in other industries.)

At a Loss?

Perhaps you're now thinking something like this: *"Wait a minute…I don't yet have the kind of quantifiable results I need in order to create a Big Idea for VITO."*

Don't let that stop you for a minute! Most VITOs will respond positively to Soft value as well as Hard value. If you need to focus on the Soft value for now, do that. And if you don't yet have the social proof ("Five other CEOs in your industry trust us to…") don't sweat that either. Why? Because, more than any other person in the entire organization, VITOs are early adopters. They really will be open to Big Ideas that *imply or indicate* that certain desirable results could be realized. The operative word here is "desirable" – from VITO's whole-brain point of view.

Remember that you represent your entire organization. You yourself may not have customers yet…you yourself may not have VIP accounts yet…you yourself may not have all the information required to put your Big Idea together. But your sales manager almost certainly does have organizational information that will help you to create this idea. Use that information! And if you find yourself hitting a brick wall, remember that you can always appeal to your own organization's VITO for help and guidance. *Your VITO will definitely get this – so don't be afraid to ask for help!*

"You don't learn how to win by getting a 'yes' – you learn how to win by getting a 'no.'"
– David Sandler

ACTION STEP

Create a new and improved draft of your BIG IDEA FOR VITO in the space below.

CHAPTER EIGHTEEN

*"Getting interest is fine, but getting pain
will get you to the bank faster." – David Sandler*

The VITO Awards

It's all about VITO…but it all starts with you!

You and you alone must create the Big Idea that will inspire – and drive – your five great minutes with VITO.

Maybe you're wondering: What's the difference between a Big Idea and any other idea? Simple. A Big Idea is something that causes VITO to *lean into* the first few seconds of his or her interaction with you, rather than *lean away*.

You must have full and complete ownership of your very own Big Idea for VITO and you must be able to describe it extemporaneously, in your own words, without sounding as though you are a preprogrammed auto-speech application.

Having said that, we know that polishing your little gem into existence is sometimes a challenge, especially if you have never created a Big Idea before. With the aim of bridging the gap between aspiration and experience, we herewith offer a gallery of *Hall of Fame* examples on the upcoming pages that you can use to guide the process of writing, rewriting, and constantly improving your big idea. These are award-winning Big Ideas that have actually generated high-value relationships with VITO – the VITO Award winners, if you will. You can use them as models in your own process – but take this word of warning before you do:

It's critically important for you to have completed all the activities we have passed along thus far, and that you understand the essence of the Balanced Gain Equation, before you move on to the content in this chapter! If you have any doubts about any of the strategies or activities you have read thus far, take a break now and go back to fill in the blanks.

As you read what follows, bear in mind that wherever you see [words in brackets], you'll have to insert your own real, verifiable numbers and words. Please *don't* try to copy these examples verbatim…but do use them to refine and perfect the drafts you've worked so hard to create in Chapters Fourteen through Seventeen. When you feel confident that what you've come up with is as solid and concise as the examples that follow, show your draft to your sales manager or a trusted colleague, or better yet, a VITO that you know. If he/she or they agree that your Big Idea is ready for prime time… move on to Part Three of this book, in which you finally launch your campaign for five minutes of VITO's precious time.

What Actually Works – Great Beginnings for Your Big Idea

Experience has shown that there are a number of ways to begin your Big Idea that are likely to make VITO *lean into* the message. You could do worse than to start your big idea with opening words that look and sound like these:

- [Five other CEOs] in your industry trust and rely upon us to…
- [Eight other Presidents] in our industry depend upon us to…
- [3] of the top [10] law firms in [San Diego]…
- Other [businessleaders] in [life-sciences]…
- Another major [retailer] here in [Lodi]…

What Actually Works – Great Endings for Your Big Idea

Just as there are reliably captivating *openings* for your Big Idea, decades of experience have shown that there are predictably successful ways of bringing the idea in for a landing. You should strongly consider concluding your idea with phrases that follow one of these patterns:

- ...here's the team that made it possible.
- ...would you like to meet the team that made it possible?
- ...the next step? Take our call to action!

The VITO Award Winners

Once again – use what follows as models for developing your own Big Idea, not as a "script" you repeat or rewrite without thought or insight. (And be sure you see the strategy points that follow these examples before you try to use any of them.)

- [5 other CEOs] in your industry trust and rely upon us to [further improve] their key executive's abilities to produce [revenues and contain costs], typically within [90 days].
- The [Deans] of [100] [Colleges and Universities] trust and rely upon us to increase enrollment by as much as [22%]... while establishing [full state and federal compliance] within [18 months].
- Other [Presidents] in your industry trust and rely upon us to increase [new business revenue] while at the same time [shortening sales cycles within 2 months].
- [Five other Presidents] in your industry trust and depend on us to increase [cash on hand] while cutting up to [$60,000] of [annual expenses].
- [Colleges and Universities across the country] trust and rely upon us to establish [full state and federal compliance] while lowering student processing costs by as much as [50%].
- Increase the overall effectiveness of your [revenue generating employees] while saving up to [30%] of your total [operational costs]. Here's the team that made it possible in

[less than 30 days].

- In [three years], annual sales skyrocketed from [$3 million to $8 million] while I quadrupled my personal income... and cut my weekly hours from [60 to 20]. Would you like to meet the team that made that happen?

- Increase overall [effectiveness of knowledge based workers]...while cutting up to [17%] of [annual support costs]. The next step? Take our call to action.

- Further increase the overall effectiveness of your [employees] ...while saving up to [30%] on all [support costs] within [6 months]. Here's the team that did it.

- [Six out of ten of] the top [OEMs] in their market [improved margins]...while reducing a [major element] of their [operational cost] by as much as [10%]. This team led the way.

- Improve the quality of your competitive intelligence while reducing market research expenditures by up to [$90,000] annually.

- We suspect that we can help you increase annual revenue as much as [$1.2 million] while holding the line on your [marketing expenses].

- Increase Net Working Capital up to [2.1%] within [90 days] ...with no additional capital expense.

- Improve knowledge-based worker efficiency while at the same time cutting up to [17%] of [direct labor cost] within [6 months].

- Our revenue jumped [35%] in [six months], with no additional cost of sales.

- A [CEO] in your industry increased [customer retention] while cutting more than [$30,000 in fixed expenses]. Here's the team that did it in just [60 days].

- [Five other CEOs] in your industry trust and depend on us to [increase cash on hand,] while cutting up to [$60,000 of annual expense]. Would you like to meet the team that made it possible?

- Other [CEOs] in your industry rely upon us to [increase cash on hand] while cutting [annual variable cost] by as much as [$60,000.00]. Here's the team that made it possible!

- "We reduced [annual premiums] by [$80,000] while providing [full mitigation of risk] that provided even greater [compliance]. Here's the team that made it possible."
  –VITO Benefito, CEO

- "[Five of the top ten retail outlets in the US] achieved full compliance while at the same time increasing [efficiency] by the end of the [quarter]. My team can lead the way."
  –YOUR VITO'S NAME GOES HERE

Wow! Would Big Ideas like those make you stop and ask yourself, "Okay – how did they do that?" Sure.

These kinds of statements make VITOs lean into your message, rather than away from it. They form the heart of the campaign you will be launching in Part Three. But…to build a statement like the ones you just read, a Big Idea that speaks VITO's language and truly "sings," you must understand that these concise, powerful ideas are the result of certain *strategies*. To make the most of the work you've done so far, you must understand those strategies!

Take a look at them right now:

Big Idea Strategy #1
Use Hard Value Numbers and Percentages Intelligently
You'll recall that Hard value is expressed using numbers and percentages. Whenever you are expressing Hard value, use terms such as:

…by as much as [$3,000.]…

…up to [23%]…

The numbers and percentages you use should be *conservative* and *understated*. This way when and if the VITO you're approaching digs deeper into your claims, he or she will be pleasantly surprised that you have positioned yourself to *understate* and *overdeliver* on your promises.

Big Idea Strategy #2
Use Soft Value, Too

Students often ask us, "What will VITO get more excited about, Hard value or Soft value?" The answer is "Yes!" VITOs invariably appreciate both kinds of value. It's best if your Big Idea can balance both Hard and Soft value. For instance:

Increase [revenue and customer care] while cutting [fixed costs] by as much as [14%].

Big Idea Strategy #3
Stay off the "Value Roller Coaster"

Avoid taking VITO on a roller-coaster ride like this:

"Increase [revenue and customer care] while cutting [fixed costs] by as much as [14%] while improving [decision making accuracy] by as much as [70%], while reducing your time to market by as much as [120 days]."

Who can keep track of all that? Keep your Big Idea focused on just two results. The two can be any mix of Hard and Soft value; ideally, you should find a way to throw the spotlight on both.

Big Idea Strategy #4
Follow The Order of VITO

Remember that VITOs tend to look for particular results in a particular order. Of course, if you know for sure that a particular problem or issue is number one on VITO's priority list, you should give that the focus in your Big Idea. Lacking that kind of inside information, though, you should assume that VITO's priority list looks like this:

1. Increasing revenue and advancing the economics of VITO, Inc. (That definitely includes maximizing shareholder value which in turn includes prompt time-to-

value and time-to-results.)

2. Increasing the effectiveness and efficiency of revenue generating employees, mission critical employees, and mission critical processes.

3. Eliminating, reducing, or containing expenses.

4. Establishing full compliance with industry and governmental regulations (i.e., staying out of jail).

Take another look at the VITO award winning Big Ideas and you'll see that they follow this general sequence of priorities.

Big Idea Strategy #5
Ask, "Can I Quote That?"

Any Big Idea that's based on results another VITO is having lends social proof and credibility. That's why under certain circumstances it's powerful to use a direct quote from another VITO. There are some "dos" and "don'ts" to be aware of here, however:

Do:

•   Associate similar industries. "Like to like" works best. In other words, if you're creating a Big Idea for a VITO in the hospitality industry, try to reference stories that connect directly to *that* industry.

•   Use your own VITO's name if at all possible (assuming that's not a competitor with the VITO you're reaching out to). This establishes "title-to-title" credibility.

Don't:

•   Reference your target VITO's competition directly. Err on the side of being conservative when it comes to mentioning a competitor's name. It's best to use what we call a "relative ranking name drop." You saw examples of this above. Here's what it looks like: "Five of the top ten manufactures in the Pacific Northwest..."

- Stretch or fabricate your statement in any way, shape or form!
- Use quotes without getting explicit permission to do so. (You should expect the VITO you're addressing to call up the VITO you're quoting.)

Big Idea Strategy #6
Use the VITOpedia

Over the past thirty-plus years, we've kept track of the words that VITOs almost always respond well to. They're reproduced in the box on the next page, which is one of most valuable patches of real estate in this book. *Find a way to build one or more of these "power words" into your Big Idea!*

THE VITOPEDIA™

Words VITOs in any industry always love to hear or read, in rough order of popularity.

- Winning
- Results
- Value
- Speed to [revenue]
- Compression
- Un-intentional
- Un-planned
- Efficiencies
- Effectiveness
- Over-achievement
- Energized
- Superb
- Unstoppable
- Ecstatic
- Excited
- Excellent
- Vibrant
- Captivating
- Passionate
- Compelling
- Perfect
- Focused
- Extraordinary
- Brilliant
- Confident
- Empowered
- Invincible
- Driven
- Discover

Big Idea Strategy #7

Stay Away from the SEEMOREpedia

Do everything you possibly can to avoid using the following words in your Big Idea. In most cases, they will be perceived, not as VITO-speak, but as the language of Seemore, the Influencer.

THE SEEMOREPEDIA™

Don't use these words in your Big Idea if you can possibly avoid doing so.

- I
- Me
- Mine
- Might
- Perhaps
- Possibly
- Probably
- Maybe

Don't skip the Action Step at the very end of this chapter! Take *at least one full hour* to put what you've just learned into action. Tweak and refine your Big Idea before moving on to Part Three. *Do not simply copy one of the examples we've shared with you here.*

Make sure your Big Idea is all yours!

> *"Success sometimes depends more on the will to act than on being concerned about what will happen if you fail."*
> *– David Sandler*

ACTION STEP

Use the examples and the seven Big Idea
strategies you just read to create a new and
improved draft of your Big Idea for VITO.
Spend at least one hour on this activity before
you move on to Part Three.

PART THREE:
GO...

CHAPTER NINETEEN

"A winner has alternatives...a loser puts all his eggs in one basket." – David Sandler

The Five Waves

There are dozens, probably hundreds, of dumb ways to try to make your first contact with VITO. One classic dumb idea that we definitely *don't* endorse is this one: hanging out in the parking lot of VITO, Inc., and waiting until you see VITO coming out of the building, then approaching unannounced and introducing yourself. Yes, there are actually books published and training programs that try to teach people how to make "parking lot presentations," and salespeople have actually tried this. The problem is that it feels less like sales and more like stalking to us, and it's likely to feel the same way to VITO. The outcome: a call to Security, rather than five good minutes with the person you've spent all this time preparing to talk to.

Fortunately, there are also a lot of *great* ways to approach VITO and launch that all-important initial five-minute interaction. We'll look at five of these great strategies in this chapter.

Taken together, these five strategies are called The Five Waves. We chose that name because we *highly* recommend that you use all five as part of a coordinated, sequenced campaign for "launching" on VITO.

If you choose to, of course, you can condense your process to include only one, two, three, or four of the Waves. But why not implement all Five Waves for five straight weeks on your target list of VITOs... and measure what happens?

The advantage of using the Five Waves as we're about to lay it out for you is pretty simple: If one of the strategies doesn't connect, there's a good chance that something else that comes later in your Wave sequence will. You'll just keep building on the previous steps you took *until* you make contact with VITO. And, as you'll see in the chapters that follow, once you've made contact, you'll use everything you've learned from Parts One and Two of this book to conduct those first five minutes with VITO.

The Five Waves contact sequence you're about to discover has delivered great conversations with thousands of VITOs in virtually every industry you can think of. That's why we want you to try it before you reject it. Remember our agreement at the beginning of the book! Give the system an honest try.

We're about to sketch out the basic principles of the Five Waves sequence for you now. The specific tools and conversational strategies you'll be using with each Wave will be covered in future chapters.

Regardless of the industry you're targeting, you'll need to get two very important pieces of information before you can put your "Wave" in motion.

1. VITO's name.
2. VITO's Private Assistant's name.

If you don't have this information, *you can't really do anything with what follows,* so you're going to need to track this data down.

You can usually get VITO's name through publicly available channels like the website of VITO, Inc., or the Chamber of Commerce directory, or any number of other purchasable directories, or a Google search that combines the name of the company with phrases like "CEO" or "founder."

If you budget your time, you really can get quite a lot out of this process, especially the on-line search. These days, it's probably a mistake *not* to Google the VITO you're about to reach out to. If there's a recent news article or press release that prominently mentions VITO, you're definitely going to want to know about that.

By the way, if you ever run into a company where the CEO, founder, or president has obviously gone to great lengths to *avoid* being publicly identified – don't bother trying to sell to that firm! This is a classic sign of a company that's hiding something. It's almost certainly not the kind of outfit you want to do business with. (Instead, you might want to think about finding some creative way to send information about that company to your competition, anonymously, disguised as a "hot lead.")

"Okay. That all makes sense – but how the heck do I figure out the name of VITO's private assistant?"

Pick up the phone and call! Look how it's going to play out. The phone rings, and you hear...

> KIND GATEKEEPER RECEPTIONIST Who's Having a Good Day: *"Good morning, VITO Incorporated – how may I direct your call?"*

> YOU: *"This is Will Prosper – would you please tell me what your CEO, Mr. Benefito's private assistant's name is?"*

> KIND GATEKEEPER RECEPTIONIST Who's Having a Good Day: *"It's Tommie Lee."*
> YOU: *"Thanks and have a nice day!"* Click.

(Or perhaps:)

GATEKEEPER RECEPTIONIST Who's Having a Not-So-Great-Day: *"VITO Incorporated, how may I direct your call?"*

YOU: *"This is Will Prosper – would you please tell me what your CEO, Mr. Benefito's private assistant's name is?"*

GATEKEEPER RECEPTIONIST Who's Having a Not-So-Great-Day: *"Why do you want to know?"*

YOU (Tell the truth!): *"We're getting ready to send your CEO, Mr. Benefito, an important piece of correspondence, and we would like to address it to his personal assistant."*

GATEKEEPER RECEPTIONIST Who's Having a Not-So-Great-Day: *"It's Tommie Lee."*

(Or perhaps:)

GATEKEEPER RECEPTIONIST Who's Having a Bad Day: *"VITO Incorporated, how may I direct your call?"*

YOU: *"This is Will Prosper – would you please tell me what your CEO, Mr. Benefito's private assistant's name is?"*

GATEKEEPER RECEPTIONIST Who's Having a Bad Day: *"Hold on…I'll connect you and you can find out for yourself."*

Victory! The phone is now ringing on the desk of VITO's private assistant. One of four wonderful outcomes are about to take place:

Wonderful Outcome #1

You'll get dumped into Tommie's voice mail. (Great! You were after this person's name – you'll virtually always get it from the outgoing message you hear at this point. Write the name down, or at least what it sounds like. If you need to, you can call the front desk again and ask for confirmation on the spelling.)

Don't worry...we'll get to the exact words you'll say on your Voice Mail Message to Tommie in a later chapter.

Wonderful Outcome #2

Tommie will pick up. (This is great, too. We'll show you how to talk to Tommie in a future chapter.)

Wonderful Outcome #3

VITO will pick up. (Paydirt! This is what you were after all the time. By the way, VITO picks up the phone more often than you might expect. Don't worry, you'll find out how to conduct this all-important call a little later on in the book.)

Wonderful Outcome #4

You'll get dumped into VITO's voice mail. (This is known as "future paydirt!" Again, a good outcome. We'll show you how to handle this situation, too.)

Think about this for a second. Outcome #1 gives you exactly the information you're looking for – the name of the private assistant. As for Outcomes 2-4...you've just gotten a preview of something we call a "no-wave Wave!" You're getting all the benefits of the Wave, without the trouble of actually having to work through all the steps. As far as you're concerned, these outcomes should be considered the equivalent of hitting fast-forward on your CD or DVD player. Suddenly, you're in the business of bonding and building rapport! There's no letter or postcard to create, no fax to send, no e-mail to craft, and no need to kick leaflets out of a low flying aircraft over VITO's parking lot! You're communicating with the two people that really matter: either VITO or VITO's assistant, Tommie. *That's exactly where you want to be.*

You'll experience your own numbers, but it's been our personal experience that about 75% of the time, you'll get a kind Receptionist Gatekeeper who's having a pretty good day – and you'll get VITO's personal assistant's name from that source, *without* getting plugged into Wonderful Outcome #1, 2, 3, or 4. What a shame!

"Okay – What Will the Five Waves Look Like?"

Now that you've got the two pieces of information you really need, let's look at how your Five Waves strategy for generating five great minutes with VITO is going to play out in VITO's world.

Wave Number One: Correspondence and Call

We're going to show you how to create and send physical, "snail-mail" VITO Correspondence via first class mail, then follow up by phone at exactly the time you said you would in the letter. That's the first Wave.

There are pluses and minuses to each of the Five Waves. The plus here is that VITO or Tommie actually have a compelling message from you, *on paper,* that they can hold in their hands, that will make your follow-up call easier, warmer, and, every once in a while, actually expected. The minus is that your message is going to have a lot company. (Consider that the U.S. Postal Service uses 2.2 million gallons of fuel each day to deliver its vast amounts of business mail.)

Wave Number Two: Correspondence, Fax, and Call:

If Wave Number One seems to have gotten you nowhere, fear not. You'll just move on to Wave Number Two. That means you'll create a new piece of VITO Correspondence, mail it via first-class mail, and then, one hour before the time you said you were going to call, you're going to fax VITO an annotated version of the same correspondence you sent via the U.S. Mail. Then you'll follow up by phone at the precise moment you promised.

This takes a little more work up-front, because you have to figure out the right fax number and then, of course, make sure the fax gets sent on time. Is getting five minutes with VITO worth that time investment? Absolutely.

The more times you 'touch' VITO before calling, and the closer you follow the guidelines you'll start reading about in Chapter Twenty, the higher the probability that VITO will be willing and ready to take your call.

Wave Number Three: Postcard Replaces the Correspondence

No action yet with VITO? No problem. You're going to do all the steps you did in Wave Number One, only this time, you're going to be using a special postcard that is brightly colored and has an abridged version of the single-page VITO Correspondence you put together in Wave Number One. This postcard often breaks the logjam, because the postcard doesn't require an envelope that has to be opened, and it uses the proven impact of color. As a result, it may get processed faster...

Just as in Wave Number One, you will follow up by phone at precisely the time you promised in your postcard's version of your Action P.S. (You'll see what an Action P.S. is – and why it's so important – in the next chapter.)

Wave Number Four: E-mail replaces the Correspondence

Depending upon the industry VITO is in (and VITO's age) you may want to move this up in the sequence, as your very first Wave. We've left it back here at Wave Number Four because some people and industries don't respond well to unsolicited e-mail.

You'll create a subject line that says something like, "our call on Monday, May 14, at 9:30 a.m." In the body of the message, you'll re-create the VITO Correspondence. You'll make your telephone call at precisely the time you said you would.

Wave Number Five: E-presentation Replaces the Correspondence

This Wave takes the most work, which is why we've saved it for last. You may, like many of our students, choose to use it only with VITOs who have not yet responded to Waves Number One through Four.

You will put together a three-slide virtual presentation that incorporates your own voice. (Our preferred resource for this kind of presentation is called Brainshark – you can learn more about them at www.brainshark.com.) You'll send this via e-mail, using a heading like the one you used for the e-mail message. You'll then follow up by phone at precisely the time you said you would.

That's what the Five Waves look like in practice. Once you try them for five straight weeks, you'll be in a good position to customize them to match them up with your own strengths, and the specifics of your own sales territory and industries you sell to. As you consider whether the steps above constitute "too much work" (a common complaint from our students), ask yourself these two questions:

1) Is a good relationship with VITO worth this kind of effort? (ANSWER: Yep!)

2) What do you think most of your *competitors* do *wrong* when it comes to building up a great connection with VITO? (We asked many top-tier VITOs this question and they all answered the same way: "Salespeople who are trying to sell to me *give up too soon!*")

ACTION STEP

Continue on with Chapter Twenty. You're about to learn how to create the powerful correspondence that will launch your Wave sequence!

CHAPTER TWENTY

"If the competition does it, stop doing it right away." – David Sandler

All Down in Black and White

Suppose we were to make you a *guarantee* that every VITO in your sales territory would read a one-page letter from you.

Notice that we're talking, not about VITO *getting* a one-page letter...but actually *reading* a one-page letter from you, from beginning to end. And not just any one-page letter, mind you, but *the ideal one-page letter*...the one-page letter that has the power to make VITO want to talk to you and see more from you, on the double. What would you offer in return for such a guarantee?

How about a single working morning of your time? Would four hours of undivided attention and creative effort from your side be worth that kind of guarantee from our side? (How about that for a perfect example of an up-front contract?)

We thought so. If you're willing to invest that morning, strap yourself in. You're about to create the correspondence that will launch your first Wave.

Your Big Idea Correspondence

What do you think a letter capable of delivering those kinds of results could possibly say? What direct message would you want VITO to get? What *could* you write on a single sheet of letter-sized paper that would pave the way for your first five minutes with VITO?

In this chapter you'll learn how to put together a very special piece of correspondence that will yield anywhere from a 25% to an 85% success rate when it comes to winning you those five minutes with VITO. Those minutes will happen either over the telephone or in person. They will be based on the Big Idea you developed in Part Two of this book.

Don't Mess With This!

Use the advice that follows *without tinkering with it* or trying to "customize" it into something else entirely. We've been creating VITO correspondence for the past twenty-three years, and have prepared final letters for more than 3 million salespeople and the organizations they work for. The system you're about to read for developing VITO-friendly correspondence *works* – so *don't try to reinvent it.*

We have success story after success story, testimonial after testimonial, rave review after rave review, about the effectiveness of the one-page correspondence system you're about to use. Even with that track record, though, even with all that social proof, we still run into salespeople who tinker with the letter around the edges, and try to make the letter "right for them." That almost always makes it wrong for VITO!

We still hear salespeople asking, "Isn't VITO getting tired of this approach, what with all the salespeople who are using this letter format?"

Answer: No. For one thing, the contents of your letter will be different than the contents of any other salesperson's letter. That's why you've done all that work up front to develop your Big Idea – to come up with a powerful idea that is entirely your own! And for another thing, VITOs are creatures of habit. They may not like to hear that, but it's true nonetheless. VITOs really are creatures of habit when it comes to processing written information. Personal interviews with over 100 top-tier VITOs confirm that they are heavy readers of *newspapers* – you know, those old-fashioned paper-based objects that people used to buy from large, coin-operated metal boxes, or have delivered to their doorsteps every morning? Believe it or not, VITOs still read those things. In fact, for most of them, newspapers like the *Wall Street Journal* and local business papers are the news source of choice! Notice what newspapers have.

1. Eye-catching headlines.

2. Quick read formats.

3. To-the-point content with up-to-date information.

4. Opinions from well known and respected sources.

5. A clear conclusion, often with a direct or implied call to action (i.e., "consider buying this stock," or "consider avoiding that stock").

As you'll see, your VITO correspondence will tap into all five of these critical elements. If VITO *doesn't get tired of the next morning's edition of the* Wall Street Journal, *VITO is not going to get tired of the next letter using this correspondence format.*

Primary Goals

Let's get clear on what we want this letter to accomplish.

1. **We want something that can be easily *scanned* before it's read.** That means long paragraphs are out of the question...and short, to-the-point statements and bullets that are easy to understand are in.

2. **We want something immensely, directly relevant to one reader.** When it comes to VITO correspondence, one size definitely does not fit all! Each of your VITO letters must be tailored to the specifics of the industry that VITO operates in. Repeat: *You cannot write a single letter that will work for each and every VITO in your territory.*

3. **We want something that uses words and phrases that *this* VITO will easily understand.** If you have one word or phrase that VITO doesn't care about, connect with or easily understand, your letter will lose – and so will you.

4. **We want something that's easy for VITO to forward on to other people.** That's pretty much what VITOs do for a living: pass things on for other people to take action on, according to VITO's instructions. Often, a good VITO letter will be passed on immediately to a Decision Maker – with a scrawl across the top that reads something like this: "Mike – look into this and get back to me with your thoughts by 6:00 am tomorrow morning–VITO."

5. **We want something that clearly states an out come or action that can be taken by both you and VITO.** In other words, we want to lay the groundworkfor the up-front contract that will be the payoff of your first conversation.

You really can write a letter that hits *five out of five* of these objectives…every single time. That means VITO will drop everything and read your letter…even though there are lots and lots of other things to do. If that's an outcome that sounds good to you…let's get started!

An Unorthodox Format

There are two points to bear in mind here. First, the format of your correspondence is every bit as critical as the contents. And second, you should be ready to create a letter that *breaks just about every rule of business correspondence you've ever encountered*. For some people, this will be a bit of a shock. For others (notably, the VITOs we've trained) writing in this unorthodox format is kind of a liberating experience. We've already confirmed that you're a whole lot like VITO…so you now know that you're about to have some fun. But do get clear on this: Your letter will look different from everything else you've ever written – because VITO is different from everyone else.

For instance…there's no letterhead up top.

You read right. No letterhead. No logos. No slogans. No corporate branding whatsoever. No kidding!

Yes, your organization has spent lots of money developing your brand, your logo, your slogan, a whole lot of stationery, and other collateral that connects to all those things. The stationery and the collateral are wonderful for correspondence with other people, but not for correspondence with a VITO with whom you've never communicated before. Your organization's letterhead, brand, logo, and slogan can (and usually do) cause an immediate *pre-judgment* in VITO's world. And, typically it's negative pre-judgment. That's something you can't afford!

Remember, VITO's personal assistant, Tommie, opens up and sorts all VITO's mail. Guess what? If you put your company logo on either your envelope or your letter, *Tommie may never even open it,* much less place it in a place of prominence on VITO's desk. Trust us on this one. Unless you work for the IRS, FBI, or CIA…unless you're VITO's personal attorney, doctor, or you happen to be one of VITO's prime suppliers, best customers or on VITO's board of directors…no letterhead, no logos, no slogans, no corporate branding of any kind, no joke!*

Keep It to One Page

Sure. You have lots you want to say to VITO. The problem is, VITO *will not read more than one page from you,* and neither will Tommie, VITO's personal assistant. Not only will your letter take the form of one page…it will take the form of one *short* page with *lots of white space* so you have room to make annotations on it in a future Wave. (More on this later.)

Nothing Else in the Envelope

No brochures. No business cards. No key-chains. No pens. No odd-shaped object designed to get the recipient of the envelope curious about the contents. *This is not direct mail marketing.* And you don't

---

*Footnote: If for some reason having to do with industry compliance reasons, you *must by law* include your company's logo and name, then put a small version of it at the bottom of the page…*not* at the top.

want security to blow it up because they think it contains something "nasty" or "dirty."

You will put *only* a single sheet of correspondence, with writing on one side and nothing on the other side, into the envelope.

Don't Fold the Letter...Don't Use Your Company's Standard Envelope

The envelope, of course, has none of your company's logos or other markings on it. It's just a standard large white or manila envelope, typically nine inches by twelve inches.

One of the important "readership" characteristics about your VITO letter is that it must be seen by the reader in its full, uncompromised glory. The big envelope makes this possible.

You won't be putting your company name in as part of the return address on the envelope, either. Just put *your* name and your company address. If you have a suite number, drop it. Nobody is going to send you anything based on your return address, and the postal service won't care, either.

Hand-write everything that goes on the envelope. Make sure you always include VITO's title in the line under VITO's name. Don't write anything besides your address and VITO's address on the envelope. Don't use phrases like "to be opened by addressee only" or "personal and confidential." Neither is appropriate to this correspondence— unless you've got pictures to put inside! But we don't recommend that as a tactic.

Got all that? Great. Now, let's look at what goes into the letter itself.

Eye-Catching Headlines

We've already established that VITO reads newspapers. Newspapers use headlines that grab the reader's interest and intent. Your letter is going to do the same thing.

Picture a clean white piece of paper sitting in front of a VITO of choice in your sales territory. At the very top of the sheet is – *not your logo* – but a headline in nice crisp, clear, large print. What does it say? No surprises here: It's your Big Idea!

Make sure your headline:

- Is brief, direct, and to the point (just like VITO). Thirty words max!
- Uses a Balanced Gain Equation that references the element of time.
- Uses words and phrases that are going to be familiar to the VITO to whom you're writing this letter.

Again – no cookie-cutters!

Here's an example for you to compare to the work you've done on your own Big Idea headline.

Five other CEOs in your industry trust and rely upon us to increase shareholder value with a 2,000% return in just 6 months. Here's the team that made it possible.

By the way, this particular headline is based on one that has built relationships with our own VITO prospects...and has directly resulted in more than four million dollars of sales revenue.

A Quick, Easy Read Equals a Good Read!

When it comes to correspondence with VITO, less is definitely more! We must create a piece of correspondence that is a *quick and easy* read from top to bottom. There really is a predictable process for doing that, and there is some science behind it, but don't worry, we promise not only to make the science part painless but also to fit it all into a single paragraph.

Here comes that paragraph. In countries that speak and read European languages, printed pages are read from the upper left to lower right. Our eyes are trained to skip over certain areas in that pathway (such as empty spaces) without hesitation – and keep going. We're a little like a freight train when this happens; it's intuitive, super-fast reading that's actually closer to "scanning." If nothing confusing or surrealistic stops the train, we keep going until we hit a word or phrase that snags the "intentional" area of our brain, and we pick up even more speed. Then we go back and review all or part of document all over again, this time more carefully. That means the total time for a correctly written one-page document should be ninety seconds, tops. If you stay away from long paragraphs (like this one), you can hit that readability target easily.

There. The science paragraph is all over, and it didn't hurt a bit. Now all we have to remember is this: Our VITO correspondence must take advantage of these principles! Therefore, we will always:

- Use very short sentences.
- Separate each paragraph with larger than normal white-space.
- Use a bullet format.
- Incorporate charts or graphs to replace or support thoughts.
- Write each paragraph or bullet in such a way that it stands on its own.

We'll show you a perfectly formatted VITO letter in just a moment but, in the spirit of what we're doing here, we want to share one more piece of formatting information with you: *Skip the typical "inside address"* that usually shows up in the upper-left-hand corner of the standard business letter. Instead, just use VITO's name and title below the Big Idea headline.

Why? Because VITO, like everyone else, starts reading at the upper-left-hand corner of the page, and VITO's name and title is one of VITO's favorite phrases to read. Experience has proven that putting *anything else* in the upper left-hand corner is, literally, a waste of space – and VITO's precious time.

Immediately after VITO's name and title, you'll put a short salutation, followed by a tie-in paragraph that will take the concept your Big Idea headline and bring it into the body of your letter. When you write this, forget about the typical opening to a typical sales letter: "It a pleasure to be presenting our full line of Feature Dump office equipment to you and your organization, each of which includes our newest YaddaYadda 2000 internal widget measuring system…"

That's not VITO-speak! Remember, you're writing a letter to a CEO, president or owner. Look at the model for the opening of letter you *will* be writing. Wherever you see a word or number in [brackets], that's a spot where you're going to put in a word or number that accurately reflects your own situation.

"We increased shareholder wealth, margins and our corporate economics with a [2,000%] return in just [6 months] while achieving full [compliance]. Here's the team that helped make it possible!"
-- Ms. Importanta, CEO, Appleton Manufacturing

Mr. Benefito
CEO
Dear Mr. Benefito,

I know the above results may seem unbelievable and at first we doubted them, too. Although they're some other [manufacturer's] results, our team of industry experts played a major role in accomplishing them. If you feel that your business operation is experiencing any level of [unintentional inefficiencies], we may be able to help eliminate them between now and the end of this [quarter] in one or more of the following ways:

Or:

We've helped cut [time] and [expense] into extremely effective business tools for [5] other [CEOs] in the [manufacturing] industry while enhancing our customers' ability to concentrate on core competencies. We've accomplished this in one or more of the following ways:

Or:

During the past [12 years], we have worked with [29 manufacturing companies] collectively, we've been able to [increase margins and shareholder value]. Are any of the following achievements on your list of goals, plans or objectives for the [first half] of this calendar [year]? If so, the good news is that we have created a proven, repeatable process that we suspect could deliver results such as:

Bold? Yes! Assumptive? Yes! Confident? Yes! *Just like VITO!* Yes!

Let's continue. You will follow this paragraph with a series of Benefit Bullets (remember the Hard and Soft value statements you worked on?) that will *briefly* describe the possible results of working with you, and/or the results you have a proven track-record of delivering.

Important! In crafting these bullets, make sure you avoid:

- Product names and numbers
- Techno-babble
- Industry jargon
- "F" words: Features, Facts, and Figures that don't belong in the VITOpedia!

Here's a "bullet" (yeah, right) in Seemore-speak:

- Complete software compatibility our cybase XPE operating system gives you full alliance connectivity to monitor pricing moves in the larger market while supporting your current network and infrastructure without the need to replace your current organic data. With our advanced pull thru fire-wall technology your critical file vault management system remains intact while our unique firm data tm, sm, xm system works in concert with all of your current software tools and ad-hoc system-wide nodes.

News flash: VITO won't read it.

In fact, VITO won't even *look* at it, because Tommie will "file it in the circular vault" before VITO gets within a hundred yards of it. Here's what a rewrite would need to deliver before you considered including it in your letter:

- *Protect valuable market share and sustain your competitive edge by proactively identifying and responding to competitor price moves and promotional offers.*

Let's do that again. Here's some impenetrable, but all-too-common, Seemore-speak, masquerading as a bullet point:

- Human Resource solutions for all sized organizations: we believe that our fully scaleable HR/2009 system will provide all of the necessary benefit tracking and on-line support needed to sustain your overloaded HR department as it tracks and verifies hard data related to mandatory filings. Our "hire to fire" back-office systems will guarantee that mistakes presently being made by your HR personnel will be eliminated without costly recurrent training. Our put-us-on-the-spot help desk is operational M-F 8 to 5 for all support needs.

And here's the rewrite that would get through customs (read: Tommie) and capture VITO's attention:

- *Improve compliance with government regulations while ensuring all fiduciary responsibilities are met.*

Got it? Good.

After your short list of well written, brief, to-the-point benefit bullets, you'll end your VITO letter with an ending paragraph that can be either somewhat bold or poised, conservative and reserved.

It's your choice. For example, here's a somewhat bold ending paragraph:

Ms. Importanta, what does some other [manufacturer's] results have to do with you and your operation? Everything, if you determine that one or more of the results mentioned in this correspondence are relevant to your strategic initiatives for the balance of [this calendar year]. All you need to do is take my call to action.

And here's a poised, conservative and reserved ending paragraph:

Mr. Benefito, the possibility for your company to achieve similar or even greater results is difficult to determine at this point. One fact is certain: You are the one person who can initiate the call to action, and together our team of experts can quickly explore exactly what all the possibilities are.

At the very bottom of your correspondence to VITO you'll include an Action P.S. That's a brief postscript with a direct reference to the action that you are, without fail, going to take at a specific day, date and time. You will put Tommie's name in this statement, so that when Tommie scans the document, you will absolutely, positively get noticed. The postscript will read something like this:

P.S. I'll call your office on Thursday, May 14 at 9:30 AM. If this is an inconvenient time, please have Tommie inform me as to when I should make the call.

Let's take a look at the entire properly formatted VITO letter.

"We increased shareholder wealth, margins and our corporate economics with a 2,000% return in just 6 months while achieving full compliance!"

Ms. Importanta
CEO, Appleton Manufacturing

May 14, 2008

Mr. Benefito
CEO

We've helped cut time and expense into extremely effective business tools for 5 other CEOs in the manufacturing industry while enhancing our customer's ability to concentrate on core competencies. We've accomplished this in one or more of the following ways:

- Protect valuable market share and sustain your competitive edge by pro-actively identifying and responding to competitor price moves and promotional offers.
- Further comply with government regulations while ensuring all fiduciary responsibilities are met.
- Increase key employee effectiveness and retention while further enhancing your product and brand reputation in the marketplace.

Mr. Benefito, the possibility for your company to achieve similar or even greater results is difficult to determine at this point. One fact is certain, you are the one person who can initiate the call to action and together our teams of experts can quickly explore exactly what all the possibilities are.

To greater success,

Will Prosper

Will Prosper
800-777-8486

P.S. I'll call your office on Thursday, May 19 at 9:30 AM. If this is an inconvenient time please have Tommie inform me as to when I should make the call.

Yes. It's different. Yes. It may look weird to you. Yes. You're worried about how your sales manager will react to it. These reactions are all very normal – and all unnecessary. Do you remember our promise to you? We're never going to ask you to do something that we're not doing today and every day in our own sales process. This model works. Trust us.

As you may have gathered, this is the central document of your Wave campaign.

ACTION STEP

To get a look at samples of the written tools you'll be using in Waves Two through Four... Quickly move to the next page!

CHAPTER TWENTY-ONE

"You can't sell anybody anything;
they must discover they want it." – David Sandler

Using Your VITO Wave Tools

The "Wave Number One" letter you just read is the foundation of your whole VITO correspondence campaign. All the other Wave tools you'll use are variations on it. Some samples are reproduced below. In the Appendix, you'll find on-line resources to download more samples you can use as models when you're formatting your own text.

Wave Two

You'll recall that Wave Two requires faxing an annotated version of your Wave One letter, one hour before your promised call. On the next page you'll see an example of what that annotated letter, sent by fax, should look like.

"We increased shareholder wealth, margins and our corporate economics with a 2,000% return in just 6 months while achieving full compliance!"

Ms. Importanta
CEO, Appleton Manufacturing

May 14, 2008

Mr. Benefito
CEO

We've helped cut time and expense into extremely effective business tools for 5 other CEOs in the manufacturing industry while enhancing our customer's ability to concentrate on core competencies. We've accomplished this in one or more of the following ways:

- Protect valuable market share and sustain your competitive edge by pro-actively identifying and responding to competitor price moves and promotional offers.
- Further comply with government regulations while ensuring all fiduciary responsibilities are met.
- Increase key employee effectiveness and retention while further enhancing your product and brand reputation in the marketplace.

Mr. Benefito, the possibility for your company to achieve similar or even greater results is difficult to determine at this point. One fact is certain, you are the one person who can initiate the call to action and together our teams of experts can quickly explore exactly what all the possibilities are.

To greater success,

Looking forward to our conversation!

Will Prosper

Will Prosper
800-777-8486

Are either of these results on your list of goals, plans or objectives?

P.S. I'll call your office on Thursday, May 19 at 9:30 AM. If this is an inconvenient time please have Tommie inform me as to when I should make the call.

Wave Three

You'll recall that, in Wave Three, you'll use a special postcard that is brightly colored and has an abridged version of the single-page VITO Correspondence you put together. Here's what the front of it looks like:

"We increased shareholder wealth and corporate economics 2,000% return in 6 months with this team's help."

VITO Benefito, CEC

April 4, 2008

Dear Ms. Importanta,

We suspect that our ideas that have worked for 7 other CEOs in your industry ma also be able to deliver results in one or more of the following areas:

- Completely protect existing marketshare and obtain all high-margin add on business
- Obtain full compliance with government and industry regulations
- Contain all major elements of operational cost by as much as 8%

We also create measurable results in six other economic performance areas which we can discuss during our exploratory conversation.

To continued success,

Will Prosper

Will Prosper
858-278-8284

P.S. I will call your office on Wednesday May, 14 at 9:30 AM. If this is an inconvenient time please have Tommie inform me as to when I should make the call.

On the back of your postcard, just as you did on the envelope of your VITO letter, you will include *only* your name and company address. As far as VITO's address goes, make sure you include VITO's title – either alongside or directly under VITO's name. Don't write anything along the bottom half-inch of either side of your postcard. That's where the U.S. Postal Service typically puts their routing bar-code.

Wave Four

In Wave Four, you'll create a special e-mail message whose text is based on the Wave One letter you saw in the previous chapter. The subject line here is particularly important: It must reference the date and time of your call to action!

Here's a sample e-mail:

Date: May 9, 2008 16:43:44 +0700
From: "Will Prosper" <will@apperton.com>
To: "Vito Importanta" <vimportanta@vitoinc.com>
Subject: Our conversation scheduled for Wednesday May 14 at 9:30 AM Pacific Time

Dear Ms. Importanta,

As you read this email other CEOs in your industry are increasing shareholder wealth, margins and corporate economics with a 2,000% return in 6 months while at the same time achieving full compliance.

We've accomplished this in one or more of the following ways:

1. Protect valuable market share and sustain competitive advantages by pro-actively identifying and responding to competitor price moves and promotional offers. Further comply with government regulations while ensuring all fiduciary responsibilities are met.

2. Further comply with government regulations while ensuring all fiduciary responsibilities are met.

2. Increase key employee effectiveness and retention while further enhancing your product and brand reputation in the marketplace.

The possibility for your company to achieve similar or even greater results is difficult to determine at this point. One fact is certain, you are the one person who can initiate the call to action and together our teams of experts can quickly explore exactly what all the possibilities are.

Attached are specifically prepared documents for three members on your executive staff:

Attachment A: Lucy Smith, C.I.O.
Attachment B: Decimal Point, C.F.O.
Attachment C: Julie Roberts, C.O.O.

We look forward to you and your team's comments and insights to our proven, repeatable process.

To greater success,
Will Prosper
858-278-8284

P.S. I'll call your office on Thursday, May 14 at 9:30 AM. If this is an inconvenient time please have Tommie inform me as to when I should make the call.

Wave Five

In this Wave, you create a three-slide presentation that incorporates your own voice. It goes out via e-mail, using a heading just like the one you used for the e-mail message. And here's where the real fun begins. Do this – send a postcard, or FAX that has the following message on it:

A special e-presentation has been sent to you that reveals how other CEOs in your industry increase shareholder wealth, margins, and corporate economics with a 2,000% return in 6 months while at the same time achieving full compliance.

We invite you to watch it. The title of the email is:

Our conversation is scheduled for Wednesday, May 14, at 9:30 AM Pacific Time.

Now, you'll compile three Powerpoint slides and a script. Then you'll go to www.brainshark.com and sign up for their service. Once you figure out how to use their (very simple) tools, you can get ready to spend a great five minutes with VITO!

What you'll see on the next page are the slides that we've used to land large amounts of business from VITOs in the Fortune 1000. If you would like to actually watch and listen to this presentation make sure you go to the on-line assets for this chapter.

Slide Number One:

INCREASE CORPORATE ECONOMICS WITH:

Larger Entry Point Sales to 54%

Compress Time-to-Revenue by 50%

Increase High-margin Add-on Business up to 120%

Slide Number Two:

ASSETS REQUIRED:

Nine individuals from your Sales Management Team

$670,000. to $870,000. by 12/31

Full Risk Mitigation

R.O.I. Up to 2,000% in 6 Months

Slide Number Three:

SOCIAL PROOF:

Majority of the F-500

Over 15,000,000 Sales Professionals Trained

200 Facilities World-wide

Yes – this presentation is in a different language than any presentation you would put together for anyone else at VITO, Inc. It's in VITO-speak! Make sure what you put together really is this direct, assumptive, and concise – follow the topics on each of the three slides, and use no more than three incredibly tight bullets to support each heading.

By the way, the racket you'll hear in the background after you build a five-minute conversation around these slides will be the accounting department at VITO, Inc., ringing up the sale and EFT-ing your check directly to the bank.

That's it – you now have all the correspondence and communication tools you will need for the Five Waves.

Perhaps you've been wondering: What on earth are you supposed to *say* when the moment comes for you to pick up the phone and dial in to VITO as you are promising in your Action P.S.? What are you supposed to do if Tommie picks up the phone? Or, what if you get dumped into voice mail! What are you supposed to do if – gasp – *VITO* picks up the phone? (It happens more often than you might imagine!)

Relax! In the next few chapters, all of this will begin to become clear to you. We'll start showing you how to turn your Big Idea into an opening statement you can use when it's time to pick up the phone and call VITO, Inc. You'll find that it's far easier than you may have imagined. You'll also find that reaching out to VITO's office by phone is actually – fun! Who knew?

CHAPTER TWENTY-TWO

"Don't practice in front of the prospect."
— David Sandler

Five Outcomes, Eight Seconds

Show time! You've created and sent your correspondence. The hour when you promised to call VITO has rolled around. It's time to pick up the phone and start the telephone part of your Wave sequence in earnest.

The big question is: **Will VITO lean into, or away from, your message?**

And the short answer is…YES.

VITO will lean into your message *if*…

…you know your desired outcome and can clearly articulate your ideas in a way that VITO can easily understand. If you do that VITO will grant you more time and that's just what we want.

…you are "ten out of ten" on the VITO scale.

…you walk your talk, and if you communicate just like VITO would.

…you are clear on exactly what you're trying to accomplish with the call.

If those things happen…THEN the odds will be very, very good indeed that VITO will lean into your message.

The main thing you need to make all this happen is a sense of where you're going. Fortunately, there are a few critical ideas that will help you help VITO choose the right direction for the conversation.

A side note: We're looking here at the five principles that drive good voice-to-voice conversation with VITO, which means we're working, in this chapter, on the assumption that you will actually reach VITO the first time you call as opposed to getting voice mail or a gatekeeper. In fact, it's quite common for VITO to be fully expecting your call, based on that powerful Wave of correspondence you sent along! So that's what we're going to get you ready for. If you have questions along the lines of "What do I do if I reach VITO's private assistant first – or reach voice mail?" please hold those questions. You'll get the answers in due course.

The five outcomes we're about to share with you describe the *outcomes* you must have in mind for this call. If you are absolutely clear on your outcomes, you will be able to keep coming back to them when things get unsettled (which they sometimes will).

> *VITO respects people who know exactly where they're going, and will almost always listen to such people for eight straight seconds. Do a stellar job during those first eight seconds and you'll be granted more time...guaranteed.*

If you know where you're going, you've got a great shot at making the first five minutes work. If you don't know where you're going, the call will crash and burn.

These five "outcomes" have been developed after years of front-line research. They are worth looking at closely – indeed, they are worth memorizing before you even pick up the phone – because conversations with VITO tend to be quite fast-paced and structured according to VITO's whims and demands. VITO's going to keep you on your toes and test you to see whether you know a) what you're talking about, and b) what you're trying to do next. Only if VITO is satisfied on these two scores will VITO be interested in participating in the conversation.

If you study these five outcomes closely, you will always know your outcome with VITO, and will never get lost in the conversation, no matter how it shifts around.

Once you know your outcomes for the call, it will be easy, not hard, for you to regain your sense of direction in the conversation, because you will always know exactly what you're trying to accomplish on the phone. Hint: *It's not selling VITO something!*

Let's assume that you're making an approach to a new VITO you've never talked to before. This is what's referred to as white space, account acquisition, prospecting for new business, or "hunting." There are other categories of VITOs to reach out to, of course – VITOs in existing accounts are particularly important for you to connect with (often referred to as "farming" for add-on business) – but account acquisition is a more or less universal concern, so let's do a close-up on this area to get you familiar with the basic principles. Your five outcomes with this new VITO are:

1. Make a great first impression.
2. Communicate with unshakable confidence.
3. Make a direct connect with your proven or suspected value inventory and VITO's industry.
4. Establish an up-front contract about what should happen next.
5. Make a great last impression.

Those are the five outcomes for the call. They are all equally important.

You can always come back to those five outcomes, no matter how weird the conversation gets. Taken together, they constitute the compass for the call you're about to make. In the final analysis, they are probably more important than the actual words that come out of your mouth. This is because VITO respects goal orientation over almost anything else.

Let's look at each of the five outcomes right now.

1. Make a Great First Impression

In order to do this with VITO, you are going to have to forget a few pieces of sales training you may have picked up from some other sources. Some of this will, we realize, take practice if you've built up a habit of saying certain things during sales calls. Break the habits.

To make sure you make a great first impression with VITO when you pick up the phone, you will, first and foremost, forget all about icebreakers ("How are you today?" or, "How's the weather out there?") and get straight to the point. Remember that VITO considers icebreakers to be lame attempts to build rapport, and reduce "tension." VITO's not tense and simply doesn't have time for them. Skip it.

You will not try to explain the technical details of your product, service or solution. Save that for Seemore.

You will forget that you need to make a sale. VITO can smell desperation a mile away. You remember the old country song about singing like you don't need the money? That's standard operating procedure when you connect with VITO. This is not about closing a sale. This is about bonding, building rapport and building up a business relationship.

You will not mention the fact that you sent a letter, or any kind of correspondence. Asking whether VITO remembers a piece of mail or e-mail is not a great start to the conversation. Don't do it!

Perhaps most important of all, you will not try to be perfect. First of all, that's a waste of time. Second of all, VITO will disengage the instant it sounds like you're trying to be something you're not. (VITO isn't perfect, either.)

2. Communicate With Unshakable Confidence

You're already "ten out of ten" on the VITO scale. Just talk that way. Pick up the phone, take your shot, stick to what you know for sure, and remember that he who tries to fast-talk VITO is lost. You'll be fine. You were a little nervous the first time you tried to pass your driving test, too. Now how big a deal is it for you to drive a car, talk on your cell phone, and down that morning beverage – simultaneously?

VITOs have some insecurities about this process, too. They're scared stiff about wasting time with salespeople. They're concerned that you'll try to engage them in a conversation about something they don't know. We'll show you how to use your own confident, concise approach to put both of those fears to rest in the next chapter.

One more point about confidence. As it turns out, confidence is the same as having faith. And developing faith is a process that's very similar to its opposite, which is of course developing fear. *If you can be fearful about something, you can just as easily build faith about the opposite outome.* It's simply a matter of choosing what you let your brain focus on. Know that the human mind, as powerful as it is, processes a positive and a negative thought in precisely the same way: by fixating on the most dramatic ideas. For example, if you say or think to yourself, "I really don't want to blow this VITO call," your brain hears "blow this VITO call." Can you guess what's going to happen?

Similarly, if you say, "I want this call to be a massively successful VITO call." Your mind hears (and manifests) "massively successful VITO call." Fear or faith? It's your choice...always has been and always will be.

3. Make a Direct Connect With Your Proven or Suspected Value Inventory and VITO's Industry

The two key words are: "VITO's industry." VITO will want to know: "How does this apply to me and the economics of my operations and/or the wealth of my shareholders?" By the way, even if VITO, Inc. is privately held by VITO, it still has "shareholder value." It's just that VITO happens to be the only shareholder!

"The only thing you can control is
your own behavior." – David Sandler

You need to know, and be ready to talk about, the broad strokes that will show exactly how your idea connects to VITO's world. Don't try to over-research this call. Just make the connection.

Remember, VITO knows more about VITO, Inc. than you ever will. The key is to approach VITO as an informed industry thought partner would – as a trusted advisor.

4. Establish an Up-Front Contract About What Should Happen Next

You will quickly learn that these conversations are all about commitments of time, attention, and resources. That's because VITOs are action-oriented and results-oriented. As a matter of fact, you can expect those traits to show up in the very first seconds of the call. Since you know your sales process, you know what VITO needs to do next to step into your ideas and suspicions. VITO doesn't. That means VITO needs to be guided, led, and coached into the up-front contract that makes the most sense to both sides. You'll need to do this while VITO maintains control and feels like she or he is at the wheel. That's no small accomplishment! You'll start learning how to manage it in the next two chapters.

5. Make a Great Last Impression

Contrary to popular belief, you don't "only get one chance to make your first impression." You get two: one at the very *beginning* of your interaction with VITO…and one at the very end of the interaction. What you say at the end of the call matters a whole bunch, just as what you say at the beginning of the call matters.

Do the Action Step below. Then move on to Chapter Twenty-Three.

ACTION STEP

With your eyes closed, mentally review the five outcomes of a good call with VITO. If you can do it blindfolded, you're ready for the next chapter.

CHAPTER TWENTY-THREE

"Never manage numbers – manage behavior."
– David Sandler

We Have Liftoff!

From this point forward, any time you encounter something that seems a little uncomfortable to you, consider that to be a good sign…and a reason to put whatever you've just learned into action!

After all, discomfort simply means you're learning something new. Like any process you haven't followed before, reaching out directly to VITO by phone will take a little time to get used to. At first, it may feel a little strange. So did riding a bicycle the first time you tried that. With actual practice, you got better at riding the bike.

It's going to be exactly the same when it comes to calling VITO. You have to put the plan into action. Don't analyze it – *do* it.

Reading this chapter, or thinking about it, won't change your behavior on the phone. Implementing what it contains, over time, is what will get the rocket off the ground.

Three Questions

As you ponder the first-call guidelines that follow, remember that they are meant for VITO. If you run across anything that seems a little unorthodox to you now, just ask yourself these three questions:

- "Does this fit in with what I now know about VITO's leadership style?"
- "Does this fit in with what I now know about VITO's values?"
- "If VITO were communicating with another VITO, would this be appropriate?"

In all cases, the answer is going to be "Yes." So let's get started.

"What's Going To Happen When I Dial The Number?"

A well-defined and consistently followed process will always yield predictable results, and the process you're about to learn is no exception. Direct experience with tens of thousands of calls to VITOs have given us some benchmarks on what you can expect to happen when you start dialing the phone to follow up on your correspondence and Waves.

Let's start with the basics. You should make as many VITO calls as possible in any given day. We suggest that you plan to make twenty calls to the VITO prospects in your territory (every half-hour on the hour) the first day you do this. We suggest that you devote one full day of your working week to making those twenty calls and recording what happens when you make them. We can tell you that those twenty calls are going to play more or less as follows:

- Twenty percent of the time (about four of your twenty calls), VITO will actually pick up the telephone. This is a considerably higher number than most people expect, and it's the reason we're sharing the "road map" for the VITO call with you now. These four calls are what you've been doing all this work for, so make the most of them, and follow the instructions that you're about to read…no exceptions! Of the remaining sixteen or so calls…

- VITO's private assistant Tommie will pick up the phone about eight times. (You'll be learning about interactions with Tommie in a later chapter.)

- The remaining eight calls will go to VITO's voice mail. (That, too, is the topic of a later chapter.)

Your Opening Statement

Picture VITO behind his or her desk. Did you picture a busy, active, engaged, and perhaps even preoccupied person? Of course you did. Now, with that picture firmly in your mind, ask yourself: What kind of opening statement would effectively invite VITO to drop everything and engage in a conversation with you?

In other words…what is the shortest possible combination of words that would spark an interest in VITO's mind sufficient to make VITO say or think, "Tell me more!"

After all, you know that VITO isn't going to be sitting around, staring at the ceiling, waiting for your call to come in. Even if VITO is the only one in the office, you can rely on this: there's already a lot going on in VITO's world. These people do not do "reactive." They are always in action and always in motion. So – how will you get VITO's attention?

By saying the magic words: VITO's name. That's the very first thing that's going to come out of your mouth. You're going to give VITO a chance to respond, and then you're going to move directly – that is, without any icebreaker, without any flattery, without any attempt to talk about yourself or your company – yes, we said *directly* dive into your Big Idea.

You're going to talk about that Big Idea, not as though you were a salesperson eager to find some way, any way, to make quota…but as though you were what you in fact are: a fellow thought-leader who knows how and when to make good business relationships happen. The conversation should sound, not like a sales call, but like two VITOs chatting briskly and enthusiastically while seated on the same park bench.

So picture this. VITO is sitting at his or her desk. It's 7:30 am – the time you said you'd call. VITO is totally unprotected; Tommie isn't in yet. The phone rings and instinctively VITO picks it up. Let's listen in on the call.

> VITO: Good morning…VITO here…how can I help you? (Or, if VITO is having a fast-paced morning: "VITO here." Or: if VITO is having a particularly rough morning: "WHAT?" Or:"This better be important!")
>
> YOU: Ms. Importanta?
>
> VITO: Yep, that's right.

YOU: It's great to speak with you! (DO NOT talk about yourself after you use this greeting. DO NOT ask how VITO is doing. DO NOT ask VITO, "Is this a good time?" DO NOT ask whether VITO got your correspondence or remembers it. Instead, move directly into your Big Idea, even if it feels a little funny the first time you do it...and it will.)

YOU: (continued): Five other CEOs in your industry rely upon us to increase margins by as much as 4% annually, while substantially increasing federal compliance. This is Will, Will Prosper with Alliance Mutual. Ms. Importanta, what's the fastest way for us to find out if our proven process could be of greater interest to you and your team by the end of this calendar month?

VITO: How did you pull that one off in this economy? Was it this past year?

Congratulations. That's a "tell me more" response. Mission accomplished! VITO has officially "leaned in" to your first eight seconds. You are now the subject of a prime-time interview that's being hosted, not by Larry King or Katie Couric, but by VITO. Hang on tight, answer the questions, take notes and remember the five great outcomes we shared with you in the previous chapter.

By the way, VITO's "tell-me-more" response could also have sounded like this:

VITO: Hold it, hold it, hold it. Who is this again? (Give your name again, slowly—and your company name, said with pride – and then explain that you sometimes talk too fast, but that's only because you're so excited about what you've been able to do for the other CEOs in VITOs industry. Then shut up.)

Or:

VITO: You sent me a letter, right? (Yep. You did. Acknowledge this in a sentence of two words or less. Then ask VITO what he or she thought of the letter. Then shut up.) For example:

YOU: Yes…what did you think of it?

Or:

VITO: "Tell me more." (Give VITO three options to choose from. Of course, each choice will be relevant to this VITO's industry, and each will be connected to a timeline. So – Is A, B, or C, more important in VITO's world this quarter? Then shut up.)

As long as you don't hear "Not interested" or a dial tone, virtually *any* response from VITO that sounds vaguely like the ones above – including a challenge from VITO – means you have successfully launched your five minutes and passed the eight-second test. *This is easier to do than you think!*

Keep your responses brief – never more than thirty seconds, preferably less than fifteen – and use only words and phrases that you know for certain that VITO will be familiar with. Follow VITO's lead.

We've been telling you over and over again about the importance of the first eight seconds when it comes to your first conversation with VITO. Look closely at what just happened in our example call. This is what made those first eight seconds a success:

You used VITO's name

These were the very first words out of your mouth. They broke preoccupation. If you're in a crowded café and someone, somewhere, says your name, you'll stop whatever you're doing long enough to turn and try to see who is calling you. Any time you call, VITO is going to be busy doing what VITOs do. *There is no "good time to call."* Saying VITO's name breaks the preoccupation…and enables VITO to lean into your message and hear what's next.

You used a pleasantry

"It's an honor to speak to you." This phrase is so effective that we recommend that you use it verbatim as you're getting familiar with this system. Of course, you may move on to other pleasantries any time you feel comfortable doing so. Say the words with enthusiasm and make them sincere. Say them with a smile on your face.

Here are some other examples of pleasantries that work:
"…thanks for picking up the phone…"
"…thanks for taking my call…"
"…it's great to speak with the person who'll appreciate the following idea…"
"…you're just the person who'll love this idea…"

Again: If VITO wants to know your name, VITO will ask for it.

You moved immediately into your Big Idea

Typically, this is the verbal rendition of the headline that was at the top of your VITO Correspondence. Notice that the Big Idea was unique to this VITO's industry, that it featured social proof (five CEOs in VITO's industry), that it incorporated the element of time (annually) and that it featured a balanced gain equation (improving margins while increasing compliance). Look at it again.

Five other CEOs in your industry rely upon us to increase margins by as much as 4% annually, while substantially improving federal compliance within just 120 days…

If you want, your Big Idea can be based upon the balance of two Hard value results:

…increase margins by as much as 4% annually, while substantially increasing the acquisition of new markets up to 2.5% within just 120 days…

…or it can be based on the balance of two Soft value results:

…substantially increase margins and the acquisition of new markets within just 120 days…

Which one will VITO lean into more? Who knows! That's for VITO to decide. It's been our experience that what's most important here is the issue and result being addressed – and the confidence you project during the call.

You only introduced your name after you were finished introducing your Big Idea

This is one of the hardest things for salespeople to get used to, so we're emphasizing its importance every chance we get. *Don't lead the call with your name.* VITO doesn't care who you are at the beginning of the call. When you do say your name, say it like this:

"…this is Will, Will Prosper with Alliance Mutual…"

Will's smart. Will knows that it's important to say his first name twice and to say it slowly. And, he says his company name with pride. Just as VITO would say it on a call to another VITO.

Use an intelligent ending question

This gets VITO used to the idea that you are comfortable asking for up-front contracts. In the first eight seconds, your statement to VITO should have these three elements:

1. VITO's name.
2. A suggested next step (aka, up-front contract).
3. The all-important element of time.

Look again at example we shared with you.

> "Ms. Importanta, (1) what's the fastest way for us to find out if our proven process could be of greater interest to you and your team (2) by the end of this calendar month (3)?"

"No one can enter your castle without your permission."
– David Sandler

Here are some additional examples of Ending Questions that work:

>"In your opinion, what is the best way for us to pursue the topic right now?"

>(This can be extremely effective. For VITO, there is no time better than right now!)

Or:

>"Have I touched on an issue that affects your day to day goals for the balance of this fiscal quarter?"

All Together Now

Look at the complete sequence that will launch the perfect first eight seconds with VITO:

- VITO's name
- Pleasantry
- Big Idea
- Your name
- Ending Question

There's a lot more to cover...the conversation has just begun! Before we move on, though, complete the Action Step below.

ACTION STEP

Practice all elements of your first eight seconds with a specific target VITO. Make sure the elements of what you say follow the precise order laid out in this chapter. This is your Opening Statement. Say it until you can deliver it without looking at any notes or reminders.

CHAPTER TWENTY-FOUR

"You have to learn to fail to win...
it's okay to make mistakes." – David Sandler

Riding the Tiger

You've launched eight great seconds with VITO.
Now what?

The best answer to that question comes in the form of another question: What do you think the PURPOSE of that first eight seconds of the call really was?

That is: What were you trying to *do* with those eight seconds?

What's The Point?

Sometimes, when we ask people that simple-sounding question, we'll hear answers like these:

- "The goal of the opening eight seconds of the call is to establish credibility with VITO."
- "The goal of the opening eight seconds of the call is to start learning more about VITO's world."
- "The goal of the opening eight seconds of the call is to tell VITO a little about who we are."

What do you think?

If you were tempted to answer our question in any of the above ways, take a time-out; give yourself a chance to re-strategize for just a second. You're not yet listening to your inner VITO!

As far as "establishing credibility" with VITO goes, that's probably not a good goal for the first eight seconds of your relationship with this person. VITOs are, by nature, pretty unconvinced people. You may be able to build up credibility with them after they've had the chance to grill you and your team for a while and after they've seen what you're capable of taking personal responsibility for and delivering, into their world. But eight seconds into the first call, they're not going to find you – or anyone else – credible, because there's no credible evidence yet of what you can do to help VITO! (And by the way, if you considered anyone "credible" after eight seconds on the phone, you wouldn't be wearing VITO's headset.)

What about the next common answer? Eight seconds into the call, can you really expect to "learn about VITO's world?" It's not very likely, because even if VITO wanted to share something of consequence with you (which is rare at this stage of the relationship), there hasn't been enough time for VITO to do so!

What about "telling VITO a little about" who you are? Well, this may be a strategy you pursue for approaching certain other individuals in the Network of Influence and Authority, but it is definitely not the way VITOs communicate with other VITOs during sales calls. Go back and look closely at the structure of your opening statement, and think about how much work you put into structuring the Big Idea that was relevant to this VITO in this industry. Did it sound like your aim in going over all that stuff was telling VITO about your company's history, or your personal experience? Of course not. The truth is, more than any other person in the enterprise, VITO is focused on himself or herself! VITO does not care about you – so that can't be the goal for the call.

Start with Bonding and Rapport!

The real purpose of those eight seconds, as we've told you before (and were hoping you'd remember), is simply to get VITO to *lean into* your message ... as opposed to leaning away. That's another way of saying that your goal for those first eight seconds is to build up bonding and rapport with VITO.

How do you establish bonding and rapport with VITO during your call? Well, you do that by thinking, talking, and, yes, bouncing back just as VITO would during a call to another VITO!

You can establish bonding and rapport with VITO by proving that you can communicate like VITO does. VITO respects that!

The rest of your five minutes with VITO is going to solidify the initial bonding and rapport you've built up…and, eventually, translate that rapport into some information about what's happening in VITO's world. That information either will – or won't – lead you to an up-front contract that makes it clear exactly what happens next in the relationship.

You're going to get to that point of *figuring out what happens next* by *riding the tiger* that is a conversation with VITO.

Rules For Riding A Tiger
To ride this tiger, you must follow some very simple rules:

Tiger Rule #1: VITO is in charge of the conversation.

Tiger Rule #2: Refer to Rule #1.

Actually, there is another Tiger Rule you must also follow. It reads as follows: Always tell the truth, and never, ever try to tap dance your way around anything you don't know for sure. When challenged about something you don't know (and you should expect to be challenged) you will say that you don't know X, promise to find out about X and then reconnect with VITO, and then *do exactly as you have promised at the precise time you promised it.*

Why is this rule so important? Look at it this way. There are lots and lots of people in VITO's world. Some of these people know what they're talking about, and admit it when they don't know about something. Other people, on the other hand, *don't* always know what they're talking about, and try to tap-dance around things when they don't know the answer. VITO distrusts people in the second category.

Some of the people in VITO's world are straight shooters. Others talk a good game. VITO will avoid people in the second category like the plague!

Follow The Rules!
In essence, all you're really going to try to do after the first eight seconds is this: follow VITO'S lead, and tell the truth at all times.

You can begin the process of following VITO's lead by "proposing an agenda" for the call that invites VITO to revise, rewrite, and challenge your suggestion. (VITO's going to do that anyway, so you might as well initiate the opportunity.) Here's what it might sound like:

> YOU: Typically, when we reach out to other [Presidents] in your industry in a call like this, we spend about five minutes talking about X, Y, and Z. Are those major concerns for you during this [calendar month]?

You are laying down some guidelines for the conversation: identifying areas that may or may not eventually connect to pain in VITO's world – and also securing an up-front contract!

At this point, VITO will either press for more information about X, Y, or Z – you're ready for that, of course – or challenge the agenda.

> VITO: Hold it. Who said X was important? What on earth does Y have to do with anything? I don't even know what you mean by Z. What we're really concerned about this quarter at VITO, Inc. is A.

Either way, you win, because you're still on the *tiger*, still moving forward with VITO, still identifying whether or not Problem A is something your organization can actually help solve.

Pay attention. Take notes. Follow Ground Rules 1, 2, and 3. Keep moving forward on the *tiger*.

The Art of the Discussion

If VITO is engaged, but requires help moving from one element to the next, you can step in as any good *tiger* trainer would and help identify the direction. Try these proven VITO-friendly phrases:

- "…by the way…"
- "…just the other day…"
- "…while talking with…"
- "…would you believe…"

- "…could you imagine…"
- "…in thinking about…"
- "…our team…"
- "…we suspect…"

Words to Use

Here are some additional words and phrases VITO likes that will help you to direct the conversation:

Winning…Results…Value…Speed to [revenue, result, value]… Compression…Effectiveness…Over-achievement…Energized… Superb…Unstoppable…Ecstatic…Excited…Excellent…Vibrant… Captivating…Passionate…Compelling…Perfect…Focused… Extraordinary…Brilliant…Confident…Empowered…Invincible… Driven…Discover.

Phrases to Use

How do you feel about…What are your thoughts about…As you know…As you're aware…Unintentional inefficiencies … What would you like for me to do next?…What's your advice on this topic?…Let me ask you…What's your opinion about… Stop me whenever you'd like to.

Words to Avoid

I…I am with…Can't…Maybe.

Phrases to avoid

We could…We think…Did you/do you know…May I ask you…As I said…Excuse me (unless you've really done something wrong).

Putting The Jigsaw Puzzle Together

Of course, you'll be using this discussion to uncover some kind of *pain* in VITO's world. Remember that the problem or pain is like a three-piece jig-saw puzzle. One piece of the puzzle represents the problem itself. Another piece represents the reasons for the problem. And, the final piece represents the impact of the problem on VITO. *If you don't identify some kind of pain VITO actually feels, and that your organization is capable of resolving, this is not an active sales lead!*

The logical first step to uncovering pain is identifying the problem situation – the gap. Often, the situation is going to be implicit in VITO's language.

Words from VITO such as unhappy, disappointed, concerned, alarmed, hopeful, frustrated, anxious, fear, worry, and doubt are indicators of a problem situation…and potentially, pain.

Whenever you encounter such a reaction from VITO (as in, "I'm concerned about where we are in relation to the numbers that the sales team is supposed to hit this quarter") think of yourself as standing on top of an undiscovered gold mine! Start digging.

Consider using the following sequence of questions as you explore situations that could connect to VITO's problem situation and as you put the pieces of the puzzle. Taken together, these questions will help you identify the reason and the impact on VITO.

- "What do you feel is the cause of it?" (Or: "Could you give me an example of that?")
- "What have you personally put into action to remedy this situation?" (Or: "What would you like to see happen to remedy this situation?")
- "And did that meet your expectations ?" (IF IT DID…this may not be an opportunity for you. IF IT DIDN'T… you've got a reason to keep talking.)
- "How much has this situation cost you and your [operation], [shareholders], [customers], [suppliers] in the past [quarter]?"
- "How do you personally feel about that?" (Or: "How does that affect you personally?")
- "Have you decided to resolve the situation at a later date?"
- "If we could help you (eliminate your problem) by (using X strategy), what would that mean for you personally?
- "What would that give your operation an opportunity to do?"
- "How important is that between [now] and the [end of this month]?"

Painting a realistic picture completes the "pain" conversation with a "get the job done" tone, which is extremely important when you're interacting with VITO. After all – these are people who like to focus on possibilities!

What Happens Next?

A moment will come when you will want to propose – or, even better, get VITO to propose – another up-front contract. Securing this commitment from VITO is an art in itself, because it requires that you bring together lots of different strands of thought into a single course of action.

There is no one way to "get" VITO to agree to another discussion; you must make the decision together, as equals. What you say to present that decision might sound like this:

> "At this point would you rather have one of your key advisors take a closer look at this, or would you rather move forward with our conversation right now?"

Or:

> "Generally, at this point, other CEOs have asked for an in-person meeting. Would you be interested in that or would you like to suggest some other path forward in the next five days?"

Or:

> "Right now may be a good time to set up a [presentation, meeting, conversation] with the person you hold most responsible in this area…"

Or:

> "Is there a process you prefer to use to take a closer look at a new idea, or are you open to some options for moving

forward between now and the end of today?"

Or:

"It looks like (sounds like/feels like) we may be at a point where the next step would make sense...what are your thoughts as to how we can move forward within the next 45 days?"

Complete the following Action Step...then move on to Chapter Twenty-Five.

ACTION STEP

Practice saying the questions you read in this chapter until they become second nature to you. Pick one end-of-call request for an up-front contract that feels comfortable to you, and practice saying that out loud, too.

CHAPTER TWENTY-FIVE

"Worry is interest paid in advance
on borrowed trouble." – David Sandler

Who's Afraid of the Gatekeeper?

All this time, you've been wondering – what about the dreaded Gatekeeper?

What about that legion of people whose mission in life is to block you, turn you away, reject you and ask you questions that stop you dead in your tracks? What will you do, what can you do, when you hear either one of these two statements?

"VITO, Incorporated – how may I direct your call?"

Or:

"Ms. Importanta's office, this is Tommie. How may I help you?"

These two statements still terrify salespeople around the world. Why is that? Fear! Not of reality, mind you, but fear of rejection, fear of being stopped from expressing our freedom of speech, fear of not being allowed to make contact, fear of looking or feeling foolish, fear of being vulnerable, fear of _____. Whatever. You fill in the blank.

Over the years, psychologists and behavioral scientists have done a lot of research on fear. Here's a very brief, but responsible, summary of what they've concluded:

1. About 96% of what is worried about and feared never happens. Of the remaining four percent that actually happens, two percent is considerably below the danger and anxiety level we assign to it.

2. Fear (like faith) is, as we have seen, a mental state. You bring it into existence by what you choose to run through your own mind.

Let's keep going. If you take all of the best lectures, training seminars, books, audio CDs, DVDs, retreats, hypnosis, education, meditation and add together all their advice on dealing with fear...this expensive, expert advice for overcoming the debilitating effects of fear can be boiled down to a single word: *Knowledge.*

Knowledge is what dispels fear. And nowhere, we submit to you, is this advice for dealing with fear more relevant than in the case of a salesperson's interactions with VITO, Inc.'s Gatekeepers.

So let's start with some knowledge that the "topic experts" on this subject may not have shared with you. There are actually *two* different Gatekeepers you may run into on your way to VITO's office.

- The Receptionist Gatekeeper
- VITO's Private Assistant

Here's some more knowledge that will help: Very few receptionist gatekeepers *set out to be* professional receptionists! They took the job because they couldn't find what they were looking for in their career of choice. They are in that position because of necessity, not because of choice. Their days are usually very busy. You'll do best with them when you treat them with compassion and respect, and be sensitive to their (very narrow) time windows for handling each call that comes in.

Here's some more knowledge to work with: VITO's Private Assistant is at the other end of the professional spectrum. This is a highly qualified, highly intelligent professional who has been hand-picked to take on one of the most important positions in the entire organization. As a matter of fact, there are several organizations that specialize in interviewing, training, and placing Personal Assistants to CEOs, Presidents, and Owners of organizations. Face it — when top-tier headhunters are targeting these people, they're important!

The Five Indisputable Rules of Receptionist Gatekeeper Interactions

It's a fact of life. You'll need to work effectively and harmoniously with the Receptionist Gatekeepers of the world. Here are the five rules for doing so:

1. Never, ever lie about the purpose of your call. In other words, never do this:

   GATEKEEPER: "Will Ms. Importanta know what this is about?"

   SALESPERSON: "Oh yes, she requested a follow up call on the information we sent." (When in fact no information was ever sent, and VITO made no request.)

2. Never, ever say you know someone if you don't. In other words, never do this:

   GATEKEEPER: "Is Mr. Benefito going to recognize your name?"

   SALESPERSON: "Of course – we met yesterday at the Chamber of Commerce meeting." (When in fact the salesperson was sitting in the audience during Mr. Benefito's speech and never really met VITO.)

3. Never, ever ignore what you hear. Always answer a direct question. In other words, never do this:

   GATEKEEPER: "Is this a sales call?"

   SALESPERSON: "No." (Come on. Of course it's a sales call.)

4. Never, ever intentionally ask for the "wrong" person. In other words, never do this:

    GATEKEEPER: "VITO Incorporated – how may I direct your call?"

    SALESPERSON: "May I speak to your janitor?" (When you are planning to ask the janitor to connect you to VITO.)

5. Never, ever ask for anything that you can get for yourself. In other words, never do this:

    GATEKEEPER: "VITO, Incorporated – how may I direct your call?"

    SALESPERSON: "What's your CEO's name?" (You couldn't check the web site? This kind of call doesn't build rapport with Gatekeepers. It irritates them.)

Your Next Call to VITO, Inc.

Now we know what you're not going to say. You're probably wondering: What will you say?

Here's the situation: You took the time to send your VITO correspondence Wave in the form of a first-class piece of mail, a fax, or an electronic message – and now you're calling, exactly as you said you would in your Action P.S.

GATEKEEPER RECEPTIONIST: "VITO Incorporated ...how may I direct your call?'

YOU: "Would you please connect me with your CEO, Ms. Importanta? Thank you." (This response is very important. Use it as written – with the right VITO name, of course!)

GATEKEEPER RECEPTIONIST: "Is Ms. Importanta expecting your call?"

YOU: "I have us down for 8:30…and I want to be right on time. Thank you for connecting me."

This is true! Your Action P.S. stated that time, and Tommie didn't call back to reschedule the call.

At this point, the Gatekeeper Receptionist may say:

"What's the call about?"

YOU: "The call is about increasing shareholder value while at the same time achieving full compliance with industry and governmental regulations. Now, it looks like I am running a bit late. Thank you for connecting me."

Say exactly what you just read with your Big Idea plugged in. Don't experiment. Don't come up with reasons not to try this. Stick to what we've just shared with you. It works! At this point, your call will be put through to VITO's office.

Old School

GATEKEEPER RECEPTIONIST: "VITO Incorporated …how may I direct your call?"

SALESPERSON: "This is Will Perish from Action Office Equipment. Could you please tell me what your president's name is?"

GATEKEEPER RECEPTIONIST: "Why do you want to know?"

SALESPERSON: "We sell a full line of copiers and multi-functional devices and I was wondering…"

"KIND" GATEKEEPER RECEPTIONIST: "Hold on, I'll connect you with our purchasing department." (Not at all what you want…but maybe what you deserve!)

Or:

GATEKEEPER RECEPTIONIST HAVING A NOT-SO-GREAT DAY: "Our president doesn't get involved with office equipment purchases, or take calls without an appointment. Let me connect you with our HR department – they might be able to help you."

GATEKEEPER RECEPTIONIST HAVING A BAD DAY: "We've got all the copiers we need." (Click…dial-tone!)

Take all of this old stuff and put it into your personal "recycle bin." Then hit "empty!"

The Five Indisputable Rules of Interactions with VITO's Private Assistant

VITO's private assistant is one of the most important, well informed, action oriented, get-it-done-now, well connected individuals you'll find at VITO, Inc. – other than VITO, of course. This person is involved in just about everything that VITO is involved with. VITOs sometimes move from one organization to another. Do you know what they do? They take Tommie with them! Here's another common trend: VITO retires…and Tommie retires at the same time!

What does this tell you?

VITO and Tommie are a team! Treat them that way! Follow these five rules to the letter.

1. Never, ever ask for VITO. For example:

    TOMMIE: "This is Tommie – how may I help you?"

    SALESPERSON: "Is Ms. Importanta in?" (We just dismissed TOMMIE. We didn't salute their uniform! This call is now officially doomed. This salesperson will never, ever get five minutes with VITO.)

2. Never, ever ask Tommie to take a message. For example:

    TOMMIE: "This is Tommie – how may I help you?"

    SALESPERSON: "Is Mr. Benefito in?"

    TOMMIE: "No."

    SALESPERSON: "Could you take a message?" (We are acting as though Tommie works for us! We're doomed again, but this time even worse! The only person Tommie works for is VITO.)

3. Never, ever ask Tommie when VITO will be in. For example:

    TOMMIE: "This is Tommie – how may I help you?"

    SALESPERSON: "Is Ms. Importanta in?"

    TOMMIE: "No."

    SALESPERSON: "When will she be back in the office?" (For all Tommie knows, this salesperson might be a disgruntled ex-employee with an ax to grind...or just an ax, period! Tommie puts VITO's office in "lockdown" mode!)

4.   Never, ever skirt a question. For example:

TOMMIE: "This is Tommie, how may I help you?"

SALESPERSON: "Is Mr. Benefito in?"

TOMMIE: "No, he's not. Who is this, and what's the call about?"

SALESPERSON: "Does he have voice mail?" (This salespeson totally ignored a direct question. As far as Tommie is concerned, your call is over. No five minutes with VITO for you!)

5.   Never, ever sound like a behind-quota salesperson. For example:

TOMMIE: "Ms. Importanta's office – this is Tommie – how may I help you?"
SALESPERSON: "Is Ms. Importanta in?:

TOMMIE: "No. She's not. Who is this and what's your call about?"

SALESPERSON: "This is Will Perish, with Debunk software solutions, calling about our latest spy-ware, the Fire-Blocker 5300. Would VITO be available to see an on-line demo at 2:00 pm today, or would 11 am tomorrow be better?" (Will is about to get a one-way ticket to Linoleumville to have a protracted chat with Seemore!)

What DO You Say to Tommie?

Here's the easiest tactic of this entire book – and the only one you'll ever need to know when it comes to working with VITO's private assistant. It's going to take you about three seconds to learn and it's an iron-clad, totally guaranteed pathway that will lead you directly to your first five minutes with VITO. Ready?

Treat Tommie like VITO.

Whenever you hear Tommie's voice, you're effectively going to forget that VITO exists, and share with Tommie what you were about to share with VITO.

No exceptions. No asking for VITO. No asking for VITO's voice mail. No putting Tommie on the witness stand. Nothing other than giving Tommy a slightly modified version of the opening statement you had planned to give VITO.

Here it is:

> TOMMIE: "Mr. Benefito's office, this is Tommie. How may I help you?"
> YOU: "Tommie, thanks for taking my call! This is Will Prosper, with Baker & Laufer. Five other CEOs in your industry rely upon us to create greater shareholder wealth while achieving full compliance with government regulations.
>
> Is this a topic that's important to you and Mr. Benefito between now and the end of this fiscal quarter?"

This is an incredibly effective approach...so don't tinker with it. Treat Tommie like VITO!

Why does this work so well? First, Tommie already knows everything that's important to VITO, and if you took the time to send the VITO letter we talked about, *Tommie will recognize your name.* That's why you say it up front! Second, notice that you're including Tommie in the mix. ("…you and Mr. Benefito…") No other salesperson is going to do this!

Don't be a bit surprised if Tommie says something close to, "Yes, Mr. Prosper, I remember seeing your letter. Mr. Benefito has it on his desk…"

You're off and running. Treat the call exactly as you would treat a call with VITO.

Now: What if Tommie doesn't respond that way? What if Tommie doesn't have a clue if shareholder value and compliance is important to VITO? What if Tommie is new? Then you'll most likely be asked if you would like to leave a voice mail message. We'll look at that possibility in our next chapter.

For now…complete the Action Step that follows.

ACTION STEP

Review this chapter closely. Then close the book.

Write down, on a separate sheet of paper, five things you will not do when you next interact with a Receptionist Gatekeeper.

Then write down the five things you will not do when you next interact with VITO's private assistant, Tommie.

CHAPTER TWENTY-SIX

"There is no such thing as a good try."
– David Sandler

VITO Voice Mail

What's been your experience thus far with leaving Voice Mail messages? Do you get call-backs most of the time from the messages you leave? Do you leave a single message and then say to yourself, "Hey, I tried?" Or have you gotten into the habit of *not leaving messages at all...* choosing instead to call back again and again until you're lucky enough to get a live voice on the other end of the line? Have you ever, in your entire sales career, left a Voice Mail message for VITO?

It's okay. You can answer those questions honestly. You're the only one listening!

Many salespeople tell us that they've pretty much given up on leaving Voice Mail messages for their prospects and suspects. When we push a little further, we find that the vast majority of them have never even left a single message in VITO's Voice Mailbox. That's a big mistake. Why? Because leaving an effective Voice Mail message for VITO is one of the most powerful sales tools at your disposal.

What follows in this chapter is a proven Voice Mail process that, when implemented effectively, will yield something on the order of an 85% return call rate.

You read correctly. If you follow the steps you're about to read and use our Voice Mail message process on ten different VITOs, you'll eventually hear back from perhaps eight or nine of those VITOs. We're going to assume those aren't the results you're getting right now...that you're ready to find out how to make numbers like those a reality in your world…and that you're ready to read on.

The Five Non-Negotiable Principles of VITO Voice Mail

What follows is probably not how you have typically left Voice Mail messages in the past.

Lots of salespeople have short attention spans, and when an immediate payoff isn't realized – as in "How will what I am doing get me a sale within the next fifteen seconds" – we may be tempted to move on to something else. As a result, we tell ourselves, "This is a waste of time," and we either abandon the idea, or we leave a completely ineffective Voice Mail.

Is that how VITO would treat a prospect?

If we keep doing the same things – that is, if we keep leaving messages the way we have always left them, or if we leave no messages at all for VITO – we will keep getting the same results we are getting now.

Let's get started. To make that 85% return call rate happen…

1. **You must be authentic.** You must not sound like you're reading from a script. *Therefore, you will not be reading from a script.*

2. **You must deliver your message with enthusiasm.** You must sound believable. *Therefore, you must truly believe that what you have to say is for VITO's ears.*

3. **You must follow up appropriately once you leave a Voice Mail message.** *Therefore, you will set up a follow-through plan.* You won't expect to leave just one message and get a call back immediately from VITO. You won't get your feelings hurt if you don't immediately get a call back. You will be prepared to leave a series of messages. That means you're going to be making quite a lot of calls, of course, and you're going to find a way to keep track of what you're doing and when you're doing it. You'll build this follow-through into whatever calendar or scheduling system you're using now. You will not "wing it" or leave it to your memory!

4. You'll be delivering a story-line – not a single desperate plea for help in meeting your quota. *Therefore, you're going to be leaving a series of contiguous messages.* As you leave each part of the story, it will set up for the next message, and the next part of the story. To tell this story, you must know, and know intimately, exactly what your organization is doing for your existing customers in the same industry as the VITO who is on the receiving side of your Voice Mail messages. This is another one of those areas where you must have completed the "homework" that we've shared with you in the earlier portions of this book. Without it, what follows in this chapter is going to be more or less useless to you.

5. You must be ready to "piggy-back" your Voice Mail Message with other tactical approaches. *Therefore, you'll be open to using Voice Mail in concert with email, faxes, and e-presentations* you learned about in the Wave chapters.

At this stage, you're probably thinking to yourself: "Fine – I'll follow the rules. What the heck am I supposed to say?" Let's look at that now. Again, some of what you'll be doing is going to be considered "unorthodox." If you need to get a skeptical sales manager on your side, encourage him or her to read this book from beginning to end!

VITO Voice Mail Message Number One

For whatever reason, VITO doesn't answer...Tommie doesn't answer...and you find yourself being dumped into VITO's Voice Mail. What do you do? Simple. You leave a Voice Mail message that's based closely on the opening statement you were going to use if you had reached VITO or Tommie directly.

All words and phrases in [brackets] in the following examples will require your own words and phrases, based on your world. What you say should be in your own words, and should not be scripted word-for-word, but should sound a whole lot like this:

"[Ms. Importanta], this is [Will Prosper] with [Dill, Spears & Sweet]– if you were in your office to take my call this is what you would have heard...[Five other CEOs] in your industry rely upon us to [further improve their competitive edge by getting new products to market up to 50% faster while cutting operational expenses by as much as 10%]. This topic could be important to both of us...that's why you'll be hearing from me again [today] at [3:30] or if you like you can call me before then at [800-877-8486]. Thanks for listening!"

Or:

"[Ms. Importanta], this is [Will Prosper] with [Dill, Spears & Sweet] – if you were in your office to take my call this is what you would have heard...[Five other CEOs] in your industry rely upon us to [further improve their competitive edge by getting new products to market up to 50% faster while cutting operational expenses by as much as 10%]. This topic could be important to both of us...that's why you'll be hearing from me again [one week from today] on [Thursday, May 14 at 3:30 PM] or if you like you can call me before then at [800-877-8486] anytime after [3:00 PM]. Thanks for listening!"

Got it? In this first VITO Voice Mail message, you're going to be delivering your opening statement as if VITO were there to take your call. Notice that you are taking the responsibility to make another call to VITO later on that same day, or on a certain clearly specified day the following week.

Now, in the space on the next page or on a separate sheet of paper, create your own Voice Mail Message Number One:

Voice Mail Message #1:

VITO Voice Mail Message Number Two

We have had the privilege of interviewing many CEOs, Presidents and Owners of various organizations. They often tell us how amazed they are that salespeople give up after the first Voice Mail message, never to be heard from again. That's not you!

You're going to keep reaching out. What's important to remember here is that, as you do so, you won't repeat *anything* you said in your first Voice Mail message.

Of course, you'll make your next call at exactly the time you said you would at the end of your last Voice Mail message. What you say should be in your own words, and should sound a lot like this:

> "[Ms. Importanta,] this is [Will Prosper]…since my last Voice Mail message we've posted two additional achievements we made possible with an organization in your industry: [full compliance with government regulations] and [risk mitigation for wrongful termination litigations]. If either is of interest to you we can get into the details when we connect-up. Which if you like can happen [tomorrow at

1:30 pm] or at your next available time. In the meantime, you can reach me at: [800-877-8486]. Looking forward to our conversation. Thanks for listening, and have a great rest of the day."

Note that we're continuing the story line that we started in our first Voice Mail message. Here again, although we're inviting VITO to call us back, we're taking the responsibility for making the next step. Remember, VITO (or Tommie) may in fact be listening to your messages...and then forwarding them on to someone else like one of their key Decision Makers.

Now, in the space that follows or on a separate sheet of paper, create your own Voice Mail Message Number Two:

Voice Mail Message #2:

VITO Voice Mail Message Number Three

It's time to turn up the urgency factor with VITO...and begin to introduce some underlying consequence of not taking action on the value you have to offer VITO, Inc.

You might initially think that what you're about to read is a bit aggressive…but remember who's listening, and remember how VITO feels about inaction, indecisiveness, "wishy-washy" attitudes, and people who don't cut to the chase.

> "[Ms. Importanta], [Will Prosper] here with a bit of a concern…as we move into the [last part] of this [calendar quarter] it may be important to note that several of our [clients] are reporting as much as a [$80,000.00] per month savings with [no] increase in [capital expense]. [Ms. Importanta], similar or even greater results could be yours if you're in search of any level of immediate improvement in the economics of your [manufacturing operation]. If so, you can reach out to me with a return phone call at [800-777-8486] between now and the end of this business day or if you prefer you can return the fax that I just sent you. Either way… we'll be able to move forward in better quantifying precisely what results are possible for you and your operation. Thanks for listening to this rather long Voice Mail message!"

Here's where we introduce two very powerful tactics…consequence selling (also known as "the cost of not taking action"), and a fax-back form. This is a concise one-page written summary of the message you just left, complete with all your contact information, and a blank space for VITO to write in about what the way forward might look like.

Now, on the next page or on a separate sheet of paper create your own Voice Mail Message Number Three:

Voice Mail Message #3:

VITO Voice Mail Message Numbers Four through Seven

Yes, that's right. You should be prepared to leave a total of seven Voice Mail messages in all. In practice, you'll usually find that you'll get some kind of response back long before you get to number seven. Why? You're leaving great Voice Mail messages for VITO, and at that level, nothing gets ignored. Follow this short list of "Guiding Principles" when it comes time to craft your fourth, fifth, sixth and seventh Voice Mail messages to VITO.

With each new Voice Mail message, you must move the sales forward. In your "story line" you can:

- Ask questions: "…which of these three repeatable results are you most interested in between now and the end of this [month]?"

- Make statements: "…our experience shows that other [Presidents] in your industry demand and expect…"

- Make assumptions: "…let's say your current [margins] are above the [14%] average and that our process can improve that number by [2%] – would that interest you enough to have a conversation… "

Again – never, ever repeat any Voice Mail message. Always connect your current Voice Mail message to a prior one. In other words, it's okay to say something like,

- "…since the last Voice Mail message you listened to…"
- "…we haven't heard back from you, so let me continue to add value to your day…"
- "…perhaps you've been out-of-town and not been getting my messages…"
- "…if you would prefer, we could reach out to your [CIO, Jackie Movit] before the end of this week…"

Always deliver your Voice Mail message with a high degree of confidence and conviction. Remember, VITO is listening (and, most likely, forwarding) your messages on to his or her Decision Maker of choice.

Always keep track of what message you've leaving for what VITO! You don't want to be caught off-guard when you get that return call from VITO!

Before you move on to Chapter Twenty-Seven, complete the Action Step below.

ACTION STEP

Create "talking points" for VITO Voice Mail messages four through seven.

CHAPTER TWENTY-SEVEN

"Work smart, not hard." – David Sandler

Shunt Alert!

Supposedly, Yogi Berra once said,

*"If you don't know where you're going,
chances are you will end up somewhere else."*

Truer words were never spoken about the sales process. A shunt is when either VITO or Tommie points you toward someone else in the organization to talk to. A shunt is merely an attempt to send you to talk to someone else, someplace else. It definitely helps to have some idea where you're going when this takes place.

Of course, there are any number of other people in the enterprise who can try to use a shunt to try to send you on your merry way, but since you're starting at the top, we don't have to worry too much about them.

Shunts can be very good or very bad. The shunts we'll be discussing in this chapter fall into two main categories:

- Controlled shunts (that is, shunts that send you someplace you already know you want to go).
- Uncontrolled shunts (that is, the shunts that Yogi warned you about, but that you accepted anyway).

The Universal Shunt Law

> *No matter what...you'll always be shunted to the person you sound the most like.*

Controlled Shunts

The best controlled shunts are the ones you get from VITO. No one knows the organization, its goals, and its history better than VITO. No one knows who's currently being held responsible for getting important stuff done better than VITO does right now. One of your goals while you are "riding the tiger" during your conversation with VITO is to avoid this kind of statement from VITO:

"I'll need to think about who to send you to."

Or:

"I'll need to think about who should be involved with what you're suggesting."

Or even:

"It doesn't look like what you're presenting here fits into what we're currently doing in our operation."

To insure yourself against those kinds of responses, you'll want to do the *homework* necessary to deftly and tactfully point VITO toward a shunt that you thought of ahead of time.

Yes. Before you even pick up the phone, it will be to your advantage to know the names and titles of specific Decision Makers within this VITO's organization that would be best suited to further qualify, uncover pain, discuss money, fulfill, and follow-up with you and your ideas, and vice versa. Remember, as VITO, Inc. is qualifying you, you are qualifying VITO, Inc.!

These days, the names of most of VITO's key players can be found somewhere on VITO's website, or by means of a simple Google search. If you draw a blank with both of those sources, you can simply call VITO, Inc., explain that you're preparing for an upcoming call with VITO, explain the attempts you've already made to track down the information, and ask the Gatekeeper Receptionist for help in getting the information you need.

The point is, you're going into the call in a way that would make Yogi proud. Before VITO points you toward anyone in the enterprise, you're going to be prepared, and you're going to *know exactly where you want to go.*

You've got to proactively look for a point in the conversation, probably near the end of your five minutes with VITO, where you can ask VITO this powerful question:

> "If we can exceed your expectations and satisfy the requirements of [Milt Hotshot, your Vice President of Business Development], could you see yourself becoming one of our customers between now and, let's say, the end of this [month]?"

Or:

> "If we can exceed your expectations and the requirements of [Milt Hotshot, your Vice President of Business Development], could you see yourself investing [$350,000.00] between now and, let's say, the end of this [month] to realize the results we've been discussing?"

Once again – this is the first time Milt's name has entered the conversation from your lips or VITO's!

You are effectively asking VITO to agree to an up-front contract with you...to agree to be open to the possibilities of a business relationship...to agree to investing money and resources (Milt's time) if you hit all the benchmarks...and you are asking for these things up front!

Don't be frightened or hesitant about asking this! VITO expects this type of direct question. It's precisely the kind of question VITO would ask before investing a lot of time in an opportunity. VITO wouldn't think of launching his or her team into any prospect's organization unless the Approver of the sale was qualified! Frankly, VITO would be disappointed in any salesperson who *omitted* this qualifying up-front step.

When salespeople avoid this kind of question, do you know what VITO thinks? "Sure glad that person isn't on my team!" which is not the type of impression you want to leave with VITO.

Consider yourself on a job interview whenever you're in the presence of VITO. Ask smart questions, like the ones you just read. Ask them with unshakable confidence and certainty in yourself and the organization you represent. If you feel you can't pull that off, then one of two situations are in play:

- You're not seriously committed to your career in sales.
- You're uncertain about the value of your products, services or solutions and the pre-sales resources that you control.

In either case...or a combination of the two...don't be calling VITO! Instead, get ready to settle in for a nice, long stay in Linoleumville with Seemore and a one-way ticket to the Sales Graveyard.

Still with us? Great. Let's look at the three results that can happen when you ask VITO a question like this.

Possibility #1
VITO Answers "Yes."

This is the doorway to Sales Paradise! When this happens...when VITO says, "I can't see why not," "Sounds good to me," or any other variation...you don't need to ask any more questions. All you need to do is "go for the gold." DON'T ask if VITO would like you to keep him or her informed. (VITO knows all and sees all already, remember?) DON'T ask VITO to reach out to Milt and let Milt know you'll be contacting him. (That's way too close to an order – and no one gives VITO an order except a unanimous coalition of board members, the IRS, VITO's defense attorney, or VITO's spouse!)

Simply reach out to Milt. Tell Milt that VITO sent you. (Believe us, Milt's going to be all ears when you say this.) Then…get to work!

Copy VITO on all correspondence and important revelations you have with Milt. No, you don't need to ask VITO's permission for this. Just do it!

Possibility #2
VITO Answers "Maybe."

If you respond to this exactly as VITO would, you'll gain major points for asserting Equal Business Stature, bonding, and building rapport. Your answer could sound something like this:

> "Thanks for being so frank and up-front. Let me ask you what would you need to see, hear or experience about our organization for you to change that maybe into a yes in the next [60 days]?"

Pay close attention to what you hear in response. Take notes, make mental pictures, do whatever you need to do, but by all means don't miss a word of VITO's answer to this question. What you're hearing is the instruction manual for selling to this VITO and winning the business. VITO is a straight shooter. You will learn exactly what process to follow to turn this VITO into a customer.

Possibility #3
VITO Answers "No"

The relevant question is: WHAT WOULD VITO DO?

Here's what you may hear:

> "No thanks – we're all set with our current source of supply."

Many salespeople would consider this the "kiss of death" – but not you! Here's one way VITO might reply:

"Would you be interested in knowing what your current source of supply may be costing you?"

Or, if you feel more comfortable with a "softer" approach:

"Would you be interested in finding out whether your current source of supply could be costing your organization anything?"

If VITO responds with anything along the lines of "What do you mean by that crack?" – you're in business. At this point, your research swings into play. You'll need to respond with something like:

"Typically, we find that we're able to [locate and eliminate un-intentional inefficiencies] in one or more of the following areas: [revenue growth in new un-identified areas], [further cost containment in supplier relationships] and [risk avoidance in business critical decision making]. Just recently, with another [life-sciences] organization, all of this added up to more than [$73,000 per quarter]."

Or suppose VITO says this:

"No – I am not interested in moving forward."

Too many salespeople cringe at the word "no." A "no" said today is just that. In other words, it may not be a "forever no." What would VITO do? Look to the future, of course! Try this:

"When would you be ready to take a closer look?"

Or:

> "It may be too early to give you a closer look from our end also. Knowing this could be an important topic for both of us. Would you like to reconnect before the end of this calendar quarter?"

Not only will VITO answer this question directly…VITO will start wondering why more salespeople like you aren't working for VITO, Inc.

Suppose VITO says:

> "We just have too many projects at this point to consider your ideas – why don't you call me in [six months]?"

This sounds like the typical stall you may get from Influencers and Recommendors…but it's not. Why not? Because it's coming from VITO.

When VITO requests a future call, it's because VITO isn't yet associating not acting on your ideas with any level of pain they might be experiencing or might experience in the future. To quickly bring the pain into the forefront of the conversation you can use a statement like this:

> "We certainly will honor your request to call you in [six months]…we also feel a responsibility to mention that in the next six months we suspect that your [new product's marketing campaign will be unintentionally missing out on as many as 500,000 potential prospects]."

You can fill in the [brackets] with any number of Hard and/or Soft benefits. Essentially, what we're doing here is presenting the cost to VITO for a "no." (Remember all the work you did to identify the pain of not taking action?)

This is a very powerful way of validating the old saying "time is money" – and in VITO's world, it really is.

What about Tommie?

Let's imagine for a moment that Tommie, VITO's Private Assistant, picks up the phone. After you share your Big Idea, and before you can propose a controlled shunt, as outlined above, Tommie takes the initiative to shunt you to someone other than VITO. This is quite common, and it's usually a very good outcome. It shows that Tommie is engaged, understands your Big Idea, and has been empowered by VITO to make sure all such propositions are quickly routed to the appropriate Decision Maker. It's important to keep in mind the "Universal Shunt Law" we mentioned at the beginning of this chapter.

Here's what the call might sound like.

> TOMMIE: "Good morning, Ms. Importanta's office — this is Tommie."
>
> YOU: "Tommie, thanks for taking my call! This is Will Prosper, with Baker & Laufer. Five other CEOs in your industry rely upon us to create greater shareholder wealth while achieving full compliance with government regulations. Is this a topic that's important to you and Ms. Importanta between now and the end of this fiscal quarter?"
>
> TOMMIE: "Perhaps…however, it may be best for you to speak directly with our Chief Performance Officer, Ms. Maye Kitt-Happin. Hold on and I'll connect you."

Mind you, this is not a bad situation to be in. The office of the CEO is about to send you directly to a Decision Maker. That Decision Maker definitely will not ignore your call. You're working at a level in VITO's organization that's most likely several levels higher than you would normally have entered.

But…it's still an uncontrolled shunt! And if you play your cards right, and treat Tommie with the respect he or she deserves, you really can improve the quality of this shunt. Here are some guidelines you must follow if you want to create a 'controlled' shunt.

You MUST:

- Honor what Tommie suggests.
- If you possibly can, take the initiative to quickly ask a few key questions before taking the shunt.
- Answer any and every question that you may be asked by Tommie.

You must NOT:

- Question Tommie's authority.
- Answer a question Tommie asks you with another question. (But you knew that already.)

Look at how it might play out:

> YOU: "Great! Thanks for your interest! Hey, before you connect me, could you tell me a little bit about Maye?"
>
> TOMMIE: "Like what? What do you want to know?"
>
> YOU: "Well, for starters...we specialize in helping and guaranteeing that our clients achieve full compliance in 90 days or less, which mitigates the liability of board members...would you happen to know if Maye is working on that requirement between now and the end of this calendar quarter? Or would this be of greater interest to your COO, Drake Driverguy?"
>
> TOMMIE: "Hmm...Actually, no...that particular task has been given to Ms. Importanta's Advisory Board Chairperson ...maybe you should have a chat with Julia Jacobson first."

YOU: "OK. Let me ask you one more question: Would it be best if you made the introduction?"

TOMMIE: "Sure – hold on. I'll stay on the line."

For most salespeople, a conversation like this is an impossibility. That's because they don't ask themselves the all-important question: *What Would VITO Do?* Most salesepeople are too quick to take a shunt…most salespeople don't know how to slow the conversation down…and take control most…salespeople don't have the unshakable confidence necessary to ask Tommie a series of intelligent questions. But you know what? VITO has that confidence! And now you do, too!

If you do what most salespeople do, you'll get the results most salespeople get. If you do what VITO would do, you'll get the kinds of results (and the respect) that VITO gets!

With a little practice, this kind of call will become the norm for you.

You're Not Done Yet

Before the end of the business day, you will reach into your top desk drawer and pull out a beautiful, tasteful "Thank-you" card. You will write:

Tommie,

Thanks so much for your assistance introducing me to Julia. We're well on our way to determining if our proven compliance program can work for you, Ms. Importanta and your board members.

Will Prosper
Will Prosper
800-777-8486

You will then take a small piece of linen writing paper and inscribe the following by hand:

Ms. Importanta,

Tommie is a delight to work with. Your accomplishments at VITO, Inc. are no surprise with talent like that on your team.

To Your Continued Success!

Will Prosper

Will Prosper
800-777-8486

What comes next is very, very important. You will take the note, put it inside the card...put the card inside a stamped envelope... hand-address the envelope to Ms. Importanta...and drop the one envelope that contains both messages into the mail before the last pick-up of <u>that</u> day.

When that card arrives at VITO, Inc. it will be sitting on VITO's desk (unopened) when VITO sees it...opens it...and reads it. Here's what will happen next. VITO will walk over to Tommie and hand over the thank-you card, minus the note, and say something like this:

> "Good job, Tommie...thanks for being such a key team player..."

The next time you call VITO and Tommie picks up the phone it will be as if two old friends were reconnecting and having a chat.

Try it!

Uncontrolled Shunts

> "Hold on...let me put you through to Purchasing..."
>
> (Or some other place you know you don't want to go.)

If this ever happens to you, and you're wondering why, consult the nearest mirror. Somewhere along the line, you stopped thinking, talking, and acting as VITO would!

CHAPTER TWENTY-EIGHT

"Selling is a Broadway show...
played by a psychiatrist." – David Sandler

Putting It All Together

Unless you dropped in on this part of the book without reading the first twenty-seven chapters, you already know for certain that VITO thinks differently than anyone else in the enterprise. You know that VITOs have a way of looking at what everyone else is looking at, but seeing something entirely different. And you also know that this ability to see things other people don't see is one of the all-important characteristics that makes VITO, well, VITO.

This top-tier player, more that any other individual you may run into in the Network of Influence and Authority, has the ability to spot opportunities where no one else sees them, and the parallel ability to identify possible problems before they arise. That's because VITOs must take an enterprise-wide approach to every question, which means they have a lot more practice at "connecting the dots" than anyone else at VITO, Inc.

Your first five minutes with VITO will set the tone and the pace for everything else that will happen in the relationship. In this chapter, we're going to walk you through the entire Sandler Selling System, as VITO, the Very Important Top Officer experiences it...and show you which of these elements you should expect to cover during your first encounter with VITO. This will most likely take place over the phone, but the principles behind what follows will work just as well when your first encounter with VITO happens to be in-person.

Bonding and Rapport

Of course, you must not only establish bonding and rapport "up front," but also re-ignite it at every step of the way in the sales process. This is not something you "check off the list." It's a constant in every meaningful business relationship, and certainly in any relationship with VITO. Notice, first and foremost, that VITOs are, as a general but very reliable rule, master rapport-builders…and rapport-re-igniters.

You need only watch a VITO interact with his or her own people to see these remarkable rapport skills in action. We've had the honor of observing many CEOs who hired us to do some form of training or speaking for Fortune 1000-level organizations. The guiding principle we identified is this: The bigger the company, the better the bonding and rapport skills of the VITO who heads the operation! Whenever you watch one of these men or women interact with the members of a national (or global!) sales team, you'll notice two things. First, salespeople tend to crowd around VITO like moths around a light bulb on a summer night.

Second, VITO builds and sustains rapport without ever pressuring members of the sales team. You know what you hear VITO saying to these people? They don't say things like "Did you close the big deal yet?" Instead, they say things like this: "Louis, how's that new baby of yours?" "Kimberly, did you set the date for the wedding yet?" "Kevin, still hitting three under par?"

Contrary to popular belief, most VITOs are supremely approachable, and they deal with people as people. We've dealt with thousands of VITOs one-on-one over the years, and the vast majority have left us with this impression, which is worth remembering in any encounter with them:

Before anything else, VITOs are people just like you and me.

If you want to master the skills of bonding and rapport, VITO-style, the first rule is going to be to be yourself. That's

VITO's secret, by the way. Virtually every VITO who stays a VITO has learned to put people at ease simply by being comfortable enough to speak and act freely, and encouraging the other person to do likewise. When Shakespeare wrote, "To thine own self be true," he was probably thinking about VITO!

For VITO, and for all great salespeople, bonding and rapport is really about dropping the hype. It's all about showing up and being your authentic self. Forget about "mirroring" VITO or "feeding back" what VITO says…just pay close attention…stay "in the moment"…and be yourself!

Those are the "big ideas" behind bonding and rapport building, VITO-style. Now, let's get a close-up on how this affects your first *five minutes with VITO.*

During your first five minutes with VITO, you will support Bonding and Rapport by…

- *Opening confidently* and showing appropriate excitement for what you do, while at the same time…
- Not dominating the conversation, or sounding like you want to.
- Knowing when to talk and when to listen.
- Keeping an ear out for what motivates VITO.
- Asking VITO intelligent questions.
- Making intelligent comments on what VITO is saying.

This is what it might sound like:

VITO SALESPERSON: "We suspect that we can add two percentage points to your gross profits by the end of this calendar quarter with a new process – and what's more, we've got a proven strategy for putting any concerns you have about compliance to rest."

PROSPECT VITO: "Hold it, hold it…start from the top. Who is this?"

VITO SALESPERSON: "Sorry…there's just so much excitement buzzing around here, I forgot to tell you! It's Will, Will Prosper of Craswell Aerospace Manufacturing." (Little pause.)

PROSPECT VITO: "Okay, go ahead."

VITO SALESPERSON: "Can you imagine cutting $600,000 from your fixed expenses between now and the end of this year?"

What you just read is not a "script"! Nor is it a "story" you should try to get VITO to act out with you in whole or in part. It is, however, an example of one way you may be able to build up bonding and rapport with VITO…by communicating in the same way VITO would communicate with another VITO.

Up-Front Contracts

The Up-Front Contract principle enables you to maintain control of the selling process, add predictability to your actions, and guarantee that you and VITO will get to the same page…and stay on the same page. VITO doesn't initiate action without having a reason for the action or knowing what to expect as a result of the action and neither should you.

At each step of the selling process, you must each have a clear picture of what you are about to do, why you are doing it, what the intended outcome will be, and how you will accomplish that outcome. If, for instance, you schedule a subsequent meeting or phone call with VITO or one of VITO's Decision Makers, you must agree to the "what," "why," "how" and "when" of the event. Without that knowledge, how would you prepare? How would you determine if you were making progress? How would you know what to do next, or when to do it?

During your first five minutes with VITO, you will support the principle of the Up-Front Contract by...

- Establishing clear ground rules for each side's investments of time, energy, or attention.
- Never agreeing to take a step that VITO asks you to take without figuring out why you're taking the step – and what will happen if and when you do. (Again – what would VITO do?)
- Paying particular attention to the issue "what happens next" in situations where you are shunted to someone whose name you do not recognize.

This is what it might sound like:

> PROSPECT VITO: "Tell you what. Why don't you give Harry Handoff a call. He's my Vice President of Finance. He's got the ball on this issue."

> VITO SALESPERSON: "Okay. A quick question for you, before Harry spends any of his valuable time with me. If Harry really sees the value we can deliver and he reaches the point where we both feel it makes sense for us to think about working together...could you personally see making an investment in this process and our solution of somewhere between $100,000 and $200,000 by the end of this quarter?"

PROSPECT VITO: "(Little pause.) If Harry signs off on this, yes, I'd consider working with you with that timeframe and that investment."

VITO SALESPERSON: "Okay – ideally, what would you want the timeframe to be for me to connect with Harry, and when would you want to hear back from us on what we find out?"

PROSPECT VITO: "He should be available to talk about this today. Tell him I told you to call. Work with Tommie to set up a time for us to have a conference call later in the week."

Again – this is only an example of something that might happen during your five minutes on the phone with VITO – it's not a "script." It's not a continuation of the first example you read, either. This is the *kind of conversation* you should have with VITO before you invest your time and energy trying to figure out what's going on in VITO's organization.

Without an up-front contract, you run the risk of mutual mystification – a situation where neither party is fully aware of the other's intentions. This leads to misunderstandings and unfulfilled expectations...and a one-way trip to the Sales Graveyard! There is no room for mutual mystification in VITO's world...and there shouldn't be in yours, either!

The word that should come to mind when you hear or see the phrase "Up-Front-Contracts" is "equal." Here's what that connects to:

Equal Business Stature
Equal Business Investments
Equal Business Interest
Equal Business Responsibility
Equal Business Liability
Equal Business Results

Pain

What concerns VITO? What unintentional inefficiencies are keeping VITO from realizing everything VITO wants realized – when VITO wants it? What delays, disconnects, and dropped balls, right now, may be preventing VITO from overachieving on VITO, Inc.'s most critical performance benchmarks for keeping customers, stakeholders, shareholders and yes, even VITO happy?

If you have some idea about what the answers to these questions could be, and you can connect your conversation to those answers, you will be able to build your five minutes with VITO around the Pain that already exists in VITO's world.

Every VITO you'll ever meet, without exception, will have Pain. Why? Because VITOs are never happy with status quo. VITOs always want improvements. In fact, VITOs create Pain if it looks like there isn't enough Pain to go around at VITO, Inc. They do this by issuing "stretch goals" that identify new markets to approach, new products to develop and grander visions of the future to pursue.

Remove the Pain, and the goal is realized – and VITO is free to go on to set some new "stretch goal" with potential obstacles that will start a whole new round of "concerns" and generate a whole new wave of "Pain discussions" that will start with VITO and, ultimately, connect to each and every key player at VITO, Inc.

If you're not talking about what concerns VITO, what keeps VITO up at night, what's bothering VITO, what's making VITO feel stressed — whether or not you use words like "Pain" or "stress" during the conversation — then you're unlikely to get the connection, and the golden shunt, that you want.

That kind of connection, that instruction to go talk to Mr. or Ms. Decision Maker and start working on a solution, is the ideal outcome of your first five minutes with VITO!

If you make a point of asking VITO what concerns him or her about X, or what the possible implications are of overlooking Y, you position yourself as that rarest of players in VITO's world: someone who volunteers to solve the problems that are flashing insistently on VITO's radar screen. You are, in short, positioning yourself as someone who looks for Pain and finds ways to remove it from VITO's world.

Of course, you must be able to follow through on any commitments you make to VITO and everyone else at VITO, Inc. Remove the Pain, and the GAP will close between the place where VITO is today, and the place where VITO wants and needs to be in the future. Remove the Pain and VITO is happy. That's your job: to make VITO happy. That's the real purpose of each and every one of your products, services and solutions: to make VITO's Pain go away.

During your first five minutes with VITO, you will use the principle of Pain by...

- Identifying problem(s)
- Uncovering reason(s)
- Quantifying impact(s)

VITOs, as you know, are quick, "whole-brain" thinkers, and they are focused relentlessly on forward progress toward their critical goals. That means that they will experience these three individual steps in a way that no one else at VITO, Inc. does.

In conversation, you will find that, even though you may bring up these elements in the order you've just seen, VITO really will connect with all three of these aspects as one, and immediately tie them to short- and long-term goals. Once VITO engages with one of these elements – typically a problem – you will very likely notice VITO sprinting off into a discussion of the reason and the impact with little or no encouragement from you. This is because VITO has to look at all the angles.

VITOs will typically give you more information than you could possibly ask for in any one of these three areas, and they will typically connect the dots for you. Unlike others in the organization, they will show you how they think the problem connects to the reasons, and the reasons connect to the impact on the whole organization. What's more, VITOs will also give you clues as to what's really going on at VITO, Inc. to deal with the problems, the reasons, and their impact.

This is what it might sound like:

> VITO SALESPERSON: "The CEOs of 65 of the Fortune 100 rely upon us to assist in improving the economics and performance of their…"

> PROSPECT VITO: (interrupting): "Time out…I've got a call coming in from a board member…I've got to run… we'll have to do this another time!"

(We now have to try to jump start a discussion about areas that may be causing VITO Pain! Fortunately, this is easier than it may sound.)

> VITO SALESPERSON (without skipping a beat): "Okay… the next time we have a chance to chat we'll have to cover our ideas for increased new business revenue and getting every area in your operation in full compliance while cutting your costs."

(We've pushed what may be the right "Pain" buttons. We may hear a little pause, and then hear VITO say, in a much different tone of voice):

> VITO: "Alright, hold the line – give me a minute to take this call...I'll be right back."

Congratulations. You're riding the tiger! Again, please note that this is not a "script" you can expect to memorize or get VITO to recite, and it is not a roleplay that connects to the other examples you've read in this chapter.

Important note: Although it's technically *possible* to move through all the steps in your first five-minute call with VITO, it's more likely that you will spend the bulk of this call exploring the **problems,** their **reasons,** and their **impact** on VITO's world. Following VITO's lead from this point forward, and having an in-depth discussion about these three interlinked issues, is a *very good goal for the first call.*

In a perfect world, your first five minutes would end with VITO's conclusion (not yours!) that:

- There is something in the status quo that is not working and needs to be fixed.
- This problem has specific *reasons* that both you and VITO understand. (Be prepared for VITO to explain the reasons to you in depth, and to ask for your input in critiquing them.)
- This problem has an *impact* on VITO's world. (Decreasing market share, dropping stock prices, and/or slower time to market are all examples of trends that *impact* VITO.)
- There should be some sort of commitment to move forward and work on the problem now.

> *It is likely that your first well executed five-minutes with VITO will move the two of you through the Pain stage, and conclude with an Up-Front Contract that establishes what should happen next to deal with the Pain you have uncovered. That is a great place to be!*

Here's another example of how it might play out. Once again, this is not a script you should try to follow, and not a "story" or "role-play" that connects to the previous examples. It is, however, a good illustration of what might happen once you do the right work in the Pain stage.

> VITO SALESPERSON: "So – how quickly would you like to see your new product development process in full federal compliance?"

> PROSPECT VITO: (who has been talking about that compliance Pain for the last five minutes): "Ideally, no later than the end of the next calendar quarter."

> VITO SALESPERSON: "Okay. Let's work backwards. We will need one full month to implement and train your key employees. That means your CFO and CTO will need to spend about one full week with my team. Which means we'll need to have our agreements signed by three weeks from today. What exactly would you like for me to do before the end of this business day?"
> PROSPECT VITO: "I want you to work with Tommie to set up a conference call with you, me, my CFO, and my CTO before the end of play today."

You now know what you will want to accomplish during your first *Five Minutes with VITO*. Pay particular attention to the Pain stage, and be sure to review the chapter entitled *Riding the Tiger* when it comes to gathering the right information.

Let's look now at how the other steps play out in VITO's world. Once again, it's possible, but not always likely, that your first phone call with VITO could move through all of these steps. What's more likely is that you'll get a "golden shunt" to talk to someone else at VITO, Inc. about things you've worked out in broad terms with VITO.

Budget

This will be an ongoing discussion as you gather more information, and it's one you want VITO involved in if it's at all possible.

Actually, VITOs don't have budgets. They say what they want, they get what they want, and they sign the checks and they leave the rest to the "bean-counters." So let's reframe the discussion and focus in on the word *investment*, which is the preferred term VITO uses when talking about money with another VITO. This "investment" mindset is quite a bit different than conversations about the budget you've had in the past with your run-of-the-mill prospects down in Linoleumville. More than anyone else in at VITO, Inc., VITO will:

1. Look for quantifiable and definable risk(s) – and reasonable mitigation thereof.
2. Look for value beyond the typical "run of the mill" return.
3. Look for more than one way to build an annuity from any investment.
4. Place considerable emphasis on the time it takes to receive the promised return.

What does it all mean? It means VITO is as interested in qualifying you as you are in qualifying VITO. In fact, one of the nicest things about dealing with VITO is that VITO will probably ask you to identify the required investment early on in the process. That's a positive sign, of course. You should be ready and willing to respond to this request without flinching. Reference a relevant project, and give a range of how much that VITO invested. Of course, the story must be true and verifiable. (Be forewarned: VITO will probably ask for an introduction to the other VITO.) Or you can give a bracketed estimate – "You may be looking at an investment ranging from X to Y, but we'll need to know more in order to develop an accurate number for your situation. Is that range in line with your over achievement of this goal?"

Put all the cards on the table. VITO will respect that – and will let you know where you stand.

It's extremely unlikely that a VITO will invest time, effort, or energy discussing the possibility of working with you without having a good idea of the investment necessary to get the job done. So you must be ready, within your first encounter with VITO, to lay out your value proposition, identify the likely investment range, and talk about the return on investment you have a proven track record of delivering (or suspect you can deliver).

VITOs don't sell to other VITOs by pussyfooting around the "price issue." Remember, VITO's think about investments, total costs not price, and, when selling, they don't discount at the first sign of trouble. VITO knows the importance of attracting the right type of value minded customer – and so should you.

Don't postpone pricing discussions. Don't justify, defend, or try to explain your pricing. If VITO gives you static on the price you want (which is unlikely), question VITO's concern before giving any answer, or even hinting that you're prepared to lower your price. For instance: "You're concerned about our price for a reason. Would you mind sharing it with me?"

Here's another example of how your conversation might go. Once again, this is not a script you should try to follow, and not a "story" or "role-play" that connects to the previous examples.

PROSPECT VITO: "I've heard of your organization…and I've also heard that your price is too high."

VITO SALESPERSON: "Could you please define 'price'?"

PROSPECT VITO: (Slightly agitated): "Price is what I pay, of course!"

VITO SALESPERSON: (Without skipping a beat): "Well, what we've found is that our price really equates to cost of ownership and overall value. It takes into consideration… (and now the smart VITO Salesperson recites a laundry-list of the value they deliver that goes well beyond the cost of whatever they're selling.)

Decision

A selling VITO doesn't put time, energy, and effort into a presentation for another VITO without knowing for sure what the benchmarks for success are and what the potential return is going to be. And neither should you! VITOS who sell are okay with the chance that the presentation may not turn into business – they just need to know what the process is going to be for determining winners and losers!

You're selling to VITO, so you're going to take precisely the same approach. That means getting clear on what marks you're going to have to hit and exceed, and what the real-world decision process is going to be.

This requires tact, because:

- VITOs have BIG egos, and it's not a good idea to challenge that ego. Never forget that power, control and authority are extremely important to VITO!

- VITO empowers and holds others responsible to sort out a lot of stuff.
- VITOs are BIG PICTURE folks who generally don't like to get "bogged down" in the details of anything, and certainly don't appreciate anyone who tries to engage them in the details of anything.

Add it all up, and your conversations with VITO about the decision making process are going to be comparatively short and detail-free, and will usually point you toward other people who will help you fill in the blanks.

That's okay. You'll find that, if VITO is actually engaged in your process, the loose ends will typically get tied up quickly. If the loose ends don't get tied up quickly, and you can't establish clear benchmarks from the people VITO puts in charge of your newfound relationship, you'll need to circle back to VITO, get clarification, and get the job done.

Here's another example. This one shows how you can clarify something that's happening in VITO's world that will connect to the decision to buy. Once again, this is not a script you should try to follow, and not a "story" or "role-play" that connects with anything we've done so far.

> PROSPECT VITO: "I've got to get my Pacific Rim franchises in place before my competition knows what I am up to. This way, we can get the mid-market early adopters in place and spring-board from there."

> VITO SALESPERSON: "Let's put an actual date on your words, 'in-place'...this way we can begin to put together the overall game plan and ensure we're exceeding your goals."

> PROSPECT VITO: (with a sense of urgency): "Well, my best scenario would be early first quarter of next year."

VITO SALESPERSON: "So we are looking at the beginning or end of January?"

You get the picture. Once you put a few really good encounters with VITO under your belt, you'll have your own unique exchanges that will be very close to what we've been showing you here.

Fulfillment

The Fulfillment step is the outcome of the successfully completed Pain, Budget, and Decision steps – and must be the result of VITO's personal commitment to view your presentation and make a decision.

If your product, service, or solution can remedy some or all of VITO's Pain by means of an investment that has a clear payoff… and if you can present your idea in a manner that is consistent with VITO's communication style…and if what you are proposing is in keeping with what you've learned about the decision-making process at VITO, Inc…then it is appropriate to ask for a chance to demonstrate directly to VITO (and anyone else in the organization VITO feels should be a part) how your product, service, or solution can help VITO, Inc. overachieve on its goals during a specific period of time. (We are using the word "demonstrate" generically, of course. Some of the products and services our students represent just aren't "demonstratable.")

The Fulfillment step is not the place to add any other "value-added" elements, previously not discussed, in the hopes of favorably influencing VITO. Unique selling points of your product or service that you present must be limited to those that specifically address the elements of VITO's situation that were uncovered in the Pain step – nothing more and certainly nothing less.

Adding additional elements during the Fulfillment step is more likely to muddy up the waters and give VITO a reason to delay moving forward than it is to accelerate the decision. VITOs are all about making decisions! So use the Fulfillment step to "let VITO be VITO."

Your presentation, as we saw in Chapter Twenty-One, must be incredibly concise to hold VITO's attention. Any changes in what you've got to offer VITO must be dealt with prior to the presentation. Ask VITO directly if anything has changed since you last spoke. If something has changed that alters the qualification of the opportunity, or VITO's ability or willingness to make a decision, the presentation must be modified, and may have to be rescheduled or canceled entirely.

Remember, the objective of the Fulfillment step is to obtain a decision, not create a situation that can only end with VITO promising to "think it over."

Lots of interesting things can happen during a presentation, especially when VITO is in the room with other team members. Sometimes, people will pose questions to prove how smart they are to VITO. Answer the questions...but do so from VITO's perspective first!

(At some point in time during your demonstration/presentation – with VITO and several individuals from VITO's team in the room – Seemore, the Influencer, poses a question:)

> SEEMORE: "So, Will, what exactly will take place when one of your servers fail to shadow our shared partition properly, and the auto back-up sends an error signal to our host system?"

> VITO SALESPERSON (Looking directly at VITO, and saving the "tech speak" for later): "Our first priority is never to lose any source of revenue or incur any risk exposure involving the loss of company-sensitive information. Compliance is never compromised, even in the case of a false error signal."

(Now the VITO Salesperson can answer the question with a more technical spin for Seemore.)

Post-Sell

You've got the "Yes!"

You're not done yet – not by a long shot. VITO must "get" that you see this mutual opportunity as the beginning of the relationship... not the end! Here are the kinds of questions you will ask to uncover any lingering doubts that might cause the sale to unravel:

- Mr. Benefito, are you 100% comfortable with your team's decision to select us as your business partner of choice?

- Ms. Importanta, is there anything we need to revisit before putting the final touches on our agreement?

- Mr. Benefito, is there anything we didn't cover that might give you reason to have second thoughts or delay moving forward?

- Ms. Importanta, if there were one event or situation that would cause you to put everything on hold or cancel it, what would that be?

Don't just memorize the questions you've just read. Internalize them!

You are testing VITO's commitment to this new business relationship. That's what VITO would do at this point: *test the commitment!* Ask these questions with confidence – as a "ten out of ten" business ally of VITO's, which is what you now are – and you will learn *exactly* where you stand vis a vis the competition...*exactly* where the potential vulnerabilities are...and exactly what you must do now to turn this single decision into a *long-term relationship* with VITO, Inc.

EPILOGUE

"Motivation is not some mystical 'up-system;'
it is the ability to see in the present
a projection of the future you want for yourself."
– David Sandler

The Journey

Sales Paradise is more of a journey than a destination, just as your first five minutes with VITO is. We believe we are all on a journey, and that we all have the obligation to find a way to keep moving forward in the right way, the way that supports us and sustains us and allows us to improve over time, whatever our skill level is.

Now that you know what you know about VITO, let us offer you our thanks for your time and attention – and a word of warning to you as fellow sales professionals: Our greatest challenge as salespeople is not likely to be anything we encounter during a discussion with VITO – but rather our own complacency, our own (mistaken) sense that we have reached our destination. In fact, whether we are the number one performer in the organization, or the rookie just starting out, we are always on a journey to improve ourselves.

We'd like to hear about what you experience on your journey.

Stay in touch!

David Mattson - Author@sandler.com
1-800-638-5686
Anthony Parinello - Author@sellingtovito.com
1-800-777-VITO

APPENDIX

On-line Broadcast Center Resources

At this point, you most likely have questions that are specific to a current, past or future sales situation. In order to provide you with the most direct pathway to Sales Paradise possible, we've put together an on-line tool for delivering answers to your questions, as well as up-to-date information on all the critical steps to your sales success. It's called a Broadcast Center, and as a reader of this book, you've got access to it. Here's how it works.

Step #1: Fire up your computer, Blackberry™, iPhone™ or whatever…and open up a browser.

Step #2: Go directly to www.sandlerbroadcastcenter.com/VITO – and while you're at it, save this site in your Favorites or Bookmarks file.

Step #3: Enter the following:
Username: Sandler
Password: VITO

Step #4: Go directly to "Core Curriculum" and immediately take the "Guided Tour."

You just took a giant step towards Sales Paradise. Enjoy!

INDEX

Congratulations! *Five Minutes With VITO* includes a complementary seminar! Now here's your last Action Step.

ACTION STEP

Learn the lastest practical, tactical, feet-in-the street sales methods directly from your neighborhood Sandler Trainers! They're knowledgeable, friendly and informed about your local selling environment.

Three easy steps to redeem your free seminar...

1. Go to www.sandler.com, click on the SEARCH NOW button (upper right corner).

2. Enter in your zip-code.

3. Call your local Sandler Trainer, mention Five Minutes with VITO, and reserve your place!

MY NOTES

MY NOTES

MY NOTES

MY NOTES